Where I was I yet knew not;
whether on the continent or on an island;
whether inhabited or not inhabited;
whether in danger of wild beasts or not.

—ROBINSON CRUSOE

The Life and Strange Surprising Adventures of

ROBINSON CRUSOE

DANIEL DEFOE

Best Loved Books for All Ages

Selected and Edited by
The Reader's Digest Association, Inc.
Pleasantville, New York

Best Loved Books for All Ages

This condensation has been created by The Reader's Digest Association, Inc. Daniel Defoe's *The Life and Strange Surprising Adventures of Robinson Crusoe* was first published in 1719.

Cover illustration by N. C. Wyeth, courtesy of Wilmington Institute, The Wilmington Library, Wilmington, Delaware
Book design by Gretchen Schuler

ISSN 1540-708X
Library of Congress Cataloging-in-Publication Data is available.
ISBN 0-7621-8885-5

Reader's Digest and the Pegasus logo are registered trademarks of The Reader's Digest Association, Inc., Pleasantville, NY 10570
www.rd.com

PRINTED IN THE UNITED STATES OF AMERICA

Contents

The Life and Strange Surprising Adventures
of
ROBINSON CRUSOE

⊰⊱ CHAPTER 1 ⊰⊱

I WAS born in the year 1632, in the City of York, of a good family, though not of that country, my father being a foreigner of Bremen, named Kreutznaer, who settled first at Hull. He got a good estate by merchandise and, leaving off his trade, lived afterwards at York, from whence he had married my mother, whose relations were named Robinson, a very good family in that country, and after whom I was so called, that is to say, Robinson Kreutznaer; but by the usual corruption of words in England, we are now called, nay, we call ourselves, and write our name, Crusoe; and so my companions always called me.

I had two elder brothers, one of whom was lieutenant colonel to an English regiment of foot in Flanders, and was killed at the battle near Dunkirk against the Spaniards. What became of my second brother, I never knew, any more than my father and mother did know what was become of me.

Being the third son, and not bred to any trade, my head began to be filled very early with rambling thoughts. My father had given me a competent share of learning, as far as house education and a country free school generally go, and designed me for the law; but I would be satisfied with nothing but going to sea; and my inclination to this led me so strongly against the commands of my father, and the entreaties of my mother, that there seemed to be something fatal in that propensity of my nature, tending directly to the life of misery which was to befall me.

My father, a wise and grave man, called me one morning into his chamber and asked me what reasons, more than a mere wandering inclination, I had for leaving his house and my native country, where I had a prospect of raising my fortune by application and industry. He told me that mine was the middle state of fortune, which he had found by long experience was the most suited to human happiness; not exposed to the miseries and hardships of the mechanic part of mankind, and not embarrassed with the pride, luxury, ambition and envy of the upper part of mankind: he told me that kings have frequently lamented the miserable consequences of being born to great things, and wished they had been placed in the middle of the two extremes, between the mean and the great; that the wise man prayed to have neither poverty nor riches. And though, he said, he would not cease to pray for me, yet he would venture to say that if I did take this foolish step, God would not bless me; and I would have leisure hereafter to reflect upon having neglected his counsel.

I was sincerely affected with this discourse, and I resolved to settle at home. But alas! A few days wore it all off; and I took my mother, at a time when I thought her pleasanter than ordinary, and told her that my thoughts were entirely bent upon seeing the world, and my father had better give me his consent than force me to go without it; that I was now eighteen years old, which was too late to go apprentice to a trade or clerk to an attorney: that I was sure, if I did, I should run away from my master before my time was out and go to sea; and if she would speak to my father to let me make but one voyage abroad, if I came home again and did not like it, I would go no more, and I would promise by a double diligence to recover the time I had lost.

This put my mother into a great passion: she told me that my father knew too well what was my interest to give his consent to anything so much for my hurt; that for her part she would not have so much hand in my destruction; and I should never have it to say that my mother was willing when my father was not.

It was not till almost a year after this that I broke loose, though I frequently expostulated with my parents about their being so determined against what my inclinations prompted me to. But being one day at Hull, whither I went without any purpose of making an elopement at that time, and one of my companions then going to London by sea in his father's ship, and prompting me to go with them, I consulted neither father nor mother, nor so much as sent them word of it; but left them without any consideration of consequences, and in an ill hour, God knows.

On the first of September, 1651, then, I went on board a ship bound for London. The ship had no sooner got out of the Humber than the wind began to blow and the waves to rise in a most frightful manner; and as I had never been at sea before, I was inexpressibly sick in body and terrified in mind. I began now to reflect upon what I had done, and how justly I was overtaken by the judgment of Heaven, for leaving my father's house.

I expected every wave would have swallowed us up, and that every time the ship fell in the trough of the sea, we should never rise more; and I made many vows that if ever I got my foot on dry land, I would never set it into a ship again while I lived. Now I saw the goodness of my father's observations about the middle station of life and how easy, how comfortable, he had lived all his days.

These sober thoughts continued during the storm; but the next day, as the sea was calmer, I began to be a little inured to it. A charming clear evening followed; and the next morning the sun shining upon a smooth sea was, as I thought, the most delightful sight that ever I saw. To make short this sad part of my story, I forgot all my repentance and all my resolutions, winning as complete a victory over conscience as any young sinner could desire.

The sixth day of our being at sea we came into Yarmouth Roads; the wind being contrary, and blowing very hard, we were obliged to come to an anchor, and here we lay for seven or eight days. The Roads being reckoned as good as a harbor, and our ground tackle very strong, our men were unconcerned and spent the time in rest and mirth, after the manner of the sea. But the eighth day, in the morning, the wind increased, and by noon the sea went very high indeed, and we thought, once or twice, our anchor had come home; upon which our master ordered out the sheet anchor; so that we rode with two anchors ahead, and the cables veered out to the bitter end.

By this time it blew a terrible storm indeed; and I began to see terror in the faces of even the seamen themselves. Looking about, I could see that two ships that rid near us had cut their masts by the board, being deeply laden; and our men cried out that a ship which rid about a mile ahead of us was foundered.

The storm was so violent that I saw what is not often seen: the master, the boatswain, and some others, more sensible than the rest, at their prayers, and expecting every moment the ship would go to the bottom. In the middle of the night we sprang a leak, and all hands were called to pump; but in spite of our work the water increased in the hold; and though the storm began to abate a little, the master began firing guns for help. A light ship, who had rid it out just ahead of us, ventured a boat out to help us. Our men cast them a rope over the stern with a buoy to it and then veered it out a great length, which they, after great labor and hazard, took hold of, and we hauled them close under our stern and got all into their boat. It was to no purpose to think of reaching their ship; so, partly rowing and partly driving, our boat went away to the northward towards the shore.

We were about a quarter of an hour out of our ship when we saw her sink; and I must acknowledge that my heart was dead within me, partly with fright and partly with horror of mind.

The men labored at the oar and at last we all got safe on shore, though not without much difficulty, and walked afterwards on foot to Yarmouth, where we were used with great humanity and given money sufficient to carry us either to London or back to Hull.

Had I now had the sense to have gone back home, I had been happy. But my ill fate pushed me on. Having some money in my pocket, I traveled to London by land; and there had many struggles with myself what course of life I should take. As to going home, it occurred to me how I should be laughed at among the neighbors and should be ashamed to see, not my father and mother only, but even everybody else. From whence I have often since observed how irrational the common temper of mankind is, especially of youth, to that reason which ought to guide them in such cases, viz., that they are not ashamed to sin, and yet are ashamed to repent; not ashamed of the action for which they ought justly to be esteemed fools, but are ashamed of the returning, which only can make them be esteemed wise men.

In this state of life, I remained some time; and the remembrance of the distress I had been in wore off; till at last I quite laid aside the thoughts of it, and looked out for a voyage. I fell acquainted with the master of a ship, who, having had very good success on the coast of Guinea, was resolved to go there again. He, taking a fancy to me and hearing me say I had a mind to see the world, told me that if I would go the voyage with him, I should be at no expense; and if I could carry anything with me, I should have all the advantage of it that the trade would admit.

I embraced the offer, and entering into a friendship with this captain, who was an honest and plain-dealing man, I went the voyage with him, and carried about forty pounds in such toys and trifles as he directed me to buy. This forty pounds I had mustered together by the assistance of some of my relations whom I corresponded with; and who, I believe, got my father, or, at least, my mother, to contribute to my first adventure. I owe the success of this voyage to the honesty of the captain, under whom also I got a competent knowledge of navigation and learned other things that were needful to be understood by a sailor; in a word, this voyage made me both a sailor and a merchant: for I brought home five pounds nine ounces of gold dust for my adventure.

❧ CHAPTER 2 ❧

I WAS now set up for a Guinea trader; and my friend, to my great misfortune, dying soon after his return to London, I resolved to go the same voyage again; and I embarked in the same vessel with one who was his mate in the former voyage and had now got the command of the ship. This was the unhappiest voyage that ever man made; for our ship, making her course between the Canary Islands and the African shore, was surprised in the gray of the morning and captured by a Turkish rover. Three of our men were killed and the rest of us were carried prisoners into Sallee, a port belonging to the Moors.

I was kept by the captain of the rover and made his slave, being young and nimble, and fit for his business. At this surprising change of my circumstances, I was perfectly overwhelmed, and looked back upon my father's prophetic discourse, now so effectually brought to pass.

As my new master had taken me to his home, so I was in hopes he would take me with him when he went to sea again, believing that it would, sometime or other, be his fate to be taken by a Spanish or Portuguese man-of-war, and that then I should be set at liberty. But when he went to sea, he left me on shore to look after his little garden and do the common drudgery of slaves about his house; and when he came home, he ordered me to lie in the cabin to look after the ship. Here I meditated nothing but my escape and what method I might take to effect it, but for two years I never had the least encouraging prospect of putting it in practice.

Then my patron, lying at home longer than usual and having by him the longboat of our English ship, resolved that he would fit it out so we might go a-fishing in it for some days. He had a little cabin built in the middle of the longboat, with a place to stand behind it, to steer and haul home the mainsheet, and room before for a hand or two to stand and work the sails. The cabin, which lay very snug and low, had in it room for him to lie, with a slave or two, and a table to eat on, with some small lockers to put in his bread, rice and coffee.

We went frequently out with this boat, and as I was most dexterous to catch fish for him, he never went without me. It happened that he had appointed to go out in this boat with two or three Moors of some distinction in that place, and for whom he had provided extraordinarily, and had sent on board the boat a larger store of provisions than ordinary, and had ordered me to put ready three guns on board his ship, for that they designed some sport of fowling as well as fishing.

I got all things ready and waited the next morning with the boat washed clean, her ensign and pendants out, when by and by, my patron came and told me his guests had put off going and ordered me with a Moor, one of his kinsmen, and a youth to go out and catch him some fish.

This moment my former notions of deliverance darted into my thoughts, for now I was like to have a little ship at my command; and my master being gone, I prepared to furnish myself, not for a fishing business, but for a voyage.

My first contrivance was to make a pretense to speak to this Moor, to get something for our subsistence on board; for I told him we must not presume to eat of our patron's bread. He said that was true, so he brought a large basket of rusk and three jars with fresh water into the boat. I conveyed a great lump of beeswax into the boat, with a parcel of twine, a hatchet, a saw, and a hammer, all which were of great use to us afterwards, especially the wax, to make candles. Another trick I tried upon him, which he innocently came into also. "Our patron's guns are on board the boat," said I. "Can you not get a little powder and shot? It may be we may kill some alcamies [fowls like our curlews]." "Yes," says he, "I will bring some"; and he brought a great leather pouch, which held about a pound and a half of powder and another with shot, and put all into the boat. Thus furnished with everything needful, we sailed out of the port about a mile before we hauled in our sail and set us down to fish.

After we had fished some time and catched nothing, for when I had fish on my hook, I would not pull them up that he might not see them, I said to the Moor, "This will not do; we must stand farther off." He agreed and, being at the head of the boat, set the sails; and as I had the helm, I ran the boat near a league farther and then brought to, as if I would fish. Then giving the boy the helm, I stepped forward to where the Moor was, and making as if I stooped for something behind him, I took him by surprise and tossed him clear overboard into the sea. He rose immediately, for he swam like a cork, and called to me, and begged to be taken in. He swam so strong after the boat that he would have reached me very quickly, there being little wind; upon which I stepped into the cabin, and fetching one of the fowling-pieces, I presented it at him and said, "You swim well, and the sea is calm. Make the best of your way to shore, and I will do you no harm; but if you come near the boat, I will shoot you, for I am resolved to have my liberty." So he turned about and swam for the shore, and I make no doubt but he reached it with ease.

Then I turned to the boy, who was called Xury, and said, "Xury, if you will be faithful to me, I will make you a great man; but if you will not, I must throw you into the sea too." The boy swore to be faithful and to go all over the world with me.

While I was in view of the Moor that was swimming, I stood out to sea with the boat, rather stretching to northward, that they might think me gone towards the strait's mouth. But as soon as it grew dusk, I changed my course and steered directly south by east, that I might keep in with the shore; and having a fair, fresh wind and a smooth, quiet sea, I made such sail that I believe by the next afternoon, at three o'clock, when I made the land, I could not be less than one hundred and fifty miles south of Sallee, quite beyond the Emperor of Morocco's dominions.

Yet I would not come to an anchor till I had sailed in that manner five days; and then the wind shifting to the southward, I concluded that if any vessels were in chase of me, they would now have given over; so I ventured to make to the coast and came to an anchor in the mouth of a little river, I knew not what or where. I neither saw, nor desired to see, any people; the principal thing I wanted was fresh water. We came into this creek in the evening, resolving to swim on shore as soon as it was dark, but we heard such dreadful noises of the barking, roaring and howling of wild creatures, that Xury begged of me not to go on shore till day. "Well," said I, "then I will not; but it may be we may see men by day, who will be as bad to us as those lions." "Then we may give them the shoot-gun," says Xury, laughing. "Make them run wey." Such English Xury spoke by conversing among us slaves. However, I was glad to see the boy so cheerful, and I took his advice.

Next morning we hauled in the boat as near the shore as

we thought was proper, and so waded to shore, carrying only our arms and two jars for water. About a mile up the creek we found the water fresh when the tide was out; so we filled our jars and went on our way, having seen no footsteps of any human creature.

As I had been one voyage to this coast before, I knew that the Cape de Verde Islands lay not far from the coast. But as I had no instruments to take an observation, I knew not where to look for them. My hope was that if I stood along this coast till I came to the part where the English traded, I should find some of their vessels that would take us in. We made on to the southward, living very sparingly on our provisions, which began to abate very much, and going no oftener into the shore than we were obliged to for fresh water. My design in this was to make the river Gambia or Senegal: that is to say, anywhere about the Cape de Verde, where I was in hopes to meet with some European ship. I knew that all the ships from Europe, which sailed either to the coast of Guinea, or to Brazil, or to the East Indies, made this Cape or those islands; and I put the whole of my fortune upon this single point, either that I must meet with some ship or must perish.

For many days I made forward, till I saw the land run out a great length into the sea; and I kept a large offing to make this point. At length, doubling the point, I saw plainly land on the other side, to seaward; then I concluded that this was the Cape de Verde, and those islands, the Cape de Verde Islands. However, they were at a great distance, and I could not tell what I had best to do; for if I should be taken with a gale of wind, I might neither reach one nor the other.

In this dilemma, as I was very pensive, I stepped into the cabin and sat me down, Xury having the helm; when, on a sudden, the boy cried out, "Master, Master, a ship with a sail!" I jumped out of the cabin and immediately saw not only the ship, but that she was a Portuguese ship, and I stretched out to sea as much as I could, resolving to speak with them.

With all the sail I could make, I found I should not be able to come in their way; but after I had crowded to the utmost and began to despair, they saw me, by the help of their perspective glasses. I made a waft of my patron's ensign for a signal of distress, and fired a gun. Upon these signals, they brought to, and lay by for me; and in about three hours' time I came up with them.

They asked me what I was, in Portuguese, and in Spanish, and in French, but I understood none of them; but at last a Scots sailor who was on board called to me, and I answered him and told him I was an Englishman, that I had made my escape out of slavery from the Moors, at Sallee; they then bade me come on board, and very kindly took me in and all my goods.

It was an inexpressible joy to me that I was thus delivered from such a miserable condition as I was in; and I immediately offered all I had to the captain of the ship, as a return for my deliverance; but he generously told me he would take nothing from me, but that all I had should be delivered safe to me when I came to the Brazils. "For," says he, "I have saved your life on no other terms than I would be glad to be saved myself; and it may, one time or other, be my lot to be taken up in the same condition. Besides," said he, "when I carry you to the Brazils, so great a way from your own country, if I should take from you what you have, you will be starved there, and then I only take away that life I had given. No, no, Senhor Inglez [Mr. Englishman]," says he, "I will carry you thither in charity, and these things will help to buy your subsistence there and your passage home again."

⤜HI CHAPTER 3 ⥞

As HE was charitable in this proposal, so he was just in the performance, for he ordered the seamen that none should touch anything I had; then he took everything into his own possession and gave me back an exact inventory of them, that I might have them, even so much as my three earthen jars.

As to my boat, he told me he would buy it of me for the ship's use and asked me what I would have for it. I told him he had been so generous to me in everything that I could not offer to make any price of the boat but left it entirely to him, upon which he told me he would give me a note of hand to pay me eighty pieces of eight for it at Brazil. He offered me also sixty pieces of eight for my boy Xury; but I was loath to sell the poor boy's liberty, who had assisted me so faithfully in procuring my own. However, when I let the captain know my reason, he owned it to be just and said that he would give the boy an obligation to set him free in ten years if he turned Christian; upon this, and Xury saying he was willing to go to him, I let the captain have him.

We had a very good voyage to the Brazils and arrived in the Baia de Todos os Santos, or All Saints Bay, in about twenty-two days. The captain would take nothing of me for my passage, gave me twenty ducats for the leopard's skin which I had in my boat, and caused everything I had in the ship to be punctually delivered to me; and what I was willing to sell, he bought of me, such as two of my guns and a piece of beeswax; in a word, I made about two hundred and twenty pieces of eight of all my cargo, and with this stock I went on shore in the Brazils.

I had not been long here before I was recommended to the house of a good honest man, like himself, who had a plantation and a sugarhouse. I lived with him some time and acquainted myself with the manner of planting and of making sugar; and seeing how well the planters lived and how they got rich suddenly, I resolved I would turn planter among them. To this purpose, getting a kind of letter of naturalization, I purchased as much land that was uncured as my money would reach and formed a plan for my plantation and settlement.

I had a neighbor, a Portuguese of Lisbon but born of English parents, whose name was Wells, and in much such circumstances as I was. His plantation lay next to mine, and we went on very sociably together. My stock was but low, as well as his, and we rather planted for food than anything else for about two years. However, we began to increase, and our land began to come into order, so that the third year we planted some tobacco and made each of us a large piece of ground ready for planting canes in the year to come; but we both wanted help, and now I found I had done wrong in parting with my boy Xury.

But alas! For me to do wrong that never did right was no great wonder. I had no remedy but to go on; I had got into an employment quite contrary to the life I delighted in and for which I forsook my father's house and broke through all his good advice; nay, I was coming into the very middle station which my father advised me to before, and which, if I resolved to go on with, I might as well have stayed at home.

I had nobody to converse with, but now and then this neighbor; no work to be done, but by the labor of my hands; and I used to say I lived just like a man cast away upon some desolate island that had nobody there but himself. But how just has it been! And how should all men reflect that when they compare their present conditions with others that are worse, Heaven may oblige them to make the exchange and be convinced of their former felicity by their experience.

The next year I raised fifty great rolls of tobacco on my own ground; and now, increasing in wealth, my head began to be full of projects beyond my reach, such as are often the ruin of the best heads in business. Had I continued in the station I was now in, I had room for all the happy things to have yet befallen me, which my father had described the middle station of life to be full of; but I was still to be the willful agent of my own miseries.

As I had once done thus in breaking away from my parents, so I must now go and leave the happy view I had of being a rich man in my new plantation, only to pursue a rash desire of rising faster than the nature of the thing admitted. To come then to the particulars of this part of my story. After having now lived almost four years in the Brazils and beginning to prosper, I had not only learned the language but had contracted an acquaintance among my fellow planters. In my discourses among them I had frequently given them an account of my two voyages to the coast of Guinea, and how easy it was to purchase on the coast for trifles—such as beads, toys, knives, scissors, hatchets, bits of glass and the like—not only gold dust, elephants' teeth, etc., but Negroes, for the service of the Brazils. They listened always attentively to my discourses on these heads, but especially to that part which related to the buying of Negroes.

It happened that three of my acquaintances came to me one morning, and after enjoining me to secrecy, they told me that they had a mind to fit out a ship to go to Guinea. They said that they were all straitened for servants as well as I; that they desired to make but one voyage, to bring the Negroes on shore privately and divide them among their own plantations; and the question was whether I would go their supercargo, to manage the trading part upon the coast of Guinea; and that I should have an equal share of the Negroes without providing any of the stock.

I, that was born to be my own destroyer, could no more resist the offer than I could restrain my first rambling designs, when my father's good counsel was lost upon me. I told them I would go with all my heart if they would look after my plantation in my absence, and would dispose of it to such as I should direct if I miscarried. This they all engaged to do: and I made a formal will, disposing of my effects in case of my death; making the captain of the ship that had saved my life my universal heir but obliging him to ship half of the produce to England. In short, I took all possible caution to preserve my effects and to keep up my plantation; had I used half as much prudence to look into my own interest, I had certainly never left so prosperous an undertaking and gone a voyage to sea, attended with all its common hazards.

But I was hurried on and obeyed blindly the dictates of my fancy; and accordingly, the ship being fitted out and the cargo furnished, I went on board in an evil hour again, the first of September, 1659, being the same day eight years that I went from my parents at Hull in order to act the rebel to their authority, and the fool to my own interest.

Our ship was about one hundred and twenty tons burden, carried six guns and sixteen men besides myself; we had on board no cargo, except beads, bits of glass, shells, looking glasses, knives, scissors, hatchets, and the like, for our trade with the Negroes.

The very same day I went on board, we set sail, standing away to the northward upon our own coast till we came to the height of Cape St. Augustino; from whence, keeping farther off at sea, we lost sight of land. We passed the Line in about twelve days' time and were, by our last observation, in seven degrees twenty-two minutes northern latitude when a violent hurricane took us quite out of our knowledge; it blew from the northeast in such a terrible manner that for twelve days together we could do nothing but drive and, scudding away before it, let it carry us whithersoever fate and the fury of the winds directed.

About the twelfth day, the weather abating a little, the master made an observation and found that he was in about eleven degrees north latitude but that he had been driven twenty-two degrees of longitude west from Cape St. Augustino; so that he was got upon the coast of Guiana, beyond the river Amazons, toward the river Orinoco, and began to consult with me what course he should take, for the ship was leaky and much disabled.

Looking over the charts of the seacoast of America, we concluded there was no inhabited country for us to have recourse to, till we came within the circle of the Caribbee islands, and therefore resolved to stand away for the English island of Barbados; which by keeping off to sea, to avoid the indraft of the Gulf of Mexico, we might perform in about fifteen days' sail.

With this design, we steered away N.W. by W.; but several days later a second storm came upon us, which carried us away westward and drove us out of the way of all human commerce.

In this distress, the wind still blowing very hard, one of our men, early in the morning, cried out, "Land!" We had no sooner run out of the cabin than the ship struck upon a sand, and the sea broke over her in such a manner that we were immediately driven into our close quarters, to shelter us from the foam and spray.

It is not easy for anyone who has not been in the like condition to conceive the consternation of men in such circumstances: we knew nothing upon what land it was we were driven, whether an island or the main, whether inhabited or not inhabited; and we could not hope to have the ship hold many minutes without breaking in pieces. In a word, we sat looking upon one another and expecting death every moment; and all the comfort we had was that, contrary to our expectation, the ship did not break yet, and that the master said the wind began to abate.

Now, though we thought that the wind did a little abate, yet the ship sticking too fast upon the sand for us to expect her getting off, we had nothing to do but to think of saving our lives as well as we could. We had a boat on board, but how to get her off into the sea was a doubtful thing; however, there was no room to debate, for we fancied the ship would break in pieces every minute.

The mate of our vessel laid hold of the boat, and with

the help of the rest of the men, got her flung over the ship's side; and getting all into her, we let her go and committed ourselves to God's mercy and the wild sea.

We worked at the oar towards the land, though with heavy hearts, like men going to execution; for we all knew that when the boat came nearer to the shore, she would be dashed in a thousand pieces by the breach of the sea—and indeed, as we made nearer the shore, the land looked more frightful than the sea.

After we had rowed, or rather driven, about a league and a half as we reckoned it, a mountainlike wave came rolling astern of us and overset the boat at once; and separating us, as well from the boat as from one another, gave us not time hardly to say, "O God!" for we were all swallowed up in a moment.

Nothing can describe the confusion of thought which I felt when I sunk into the water; for though I swam very well, I could not deliver myself from the waves so as to draw my breath, till that wave having carried me a vast way on towards the shore and, having spent itself, went back and left me upon the land half dead with the water I took in. I got upon my feet and endeavored to make on towards the land as fast as I could, before another wave should return and take me up again; but I soon saw the sea come after me as high as a great hill, and as furious as an enemy which I had no means or strength to contend with.

The wave that came upon me buried me twenty or thirty feet deep in its own body; and I could feel myself carried with a mighty force and swiftness towards the shore, but I held my breath and swam forward with all my might. I was ready to burst with holding my breath, when I found my head and hands shoot out above the surface of the water; and though it was not two seconds of time that I could keep myself so, yet it relieved me greatly, gave me breath and new courage. Twice more I was lifted up by the waves and carried forwards as before, the shore being very flat.

The last time of these two had well nigh been fatal to me; for the sea, having hurried me along as before, dashed me against a rock with such force that it left me senseless. The blow, taking my side and breast, beat the breath, as it were, quite out of my body. But I recovered a little before the return of the waves, and seeing I should again be covered with the water, I resolved to hold fast by a piece of the rock, and so to hold my breath till the wave went back. Now, as the waves were not so high as the first, being nearer land, I held my hold till the waves abated and then fetched another run, which brought me so near the shore that the next wave, though it went over me, yet did not so swallow me up as to carry me away; and the next run I took, I got to the mainland, where I clambered up the cliffs and sat me down upon the grass, free from danger and quite out of the reach of the water.

I now began to look up and thank God that my life was saved, in a case wherein there was, some minutes before, scarcely any room to hope. I walked about, lifting up my hands, and my whole being, as I may say, wrapped up in the contemplation of my deliverance; making a thousand gestures and motions which I cannot describe; reflecting upon my comrades that were drowned, and that there should not be one soul saved but myself; for I never saw them afterwards, or any sign of them, except three of their hats, one cap, and two shoes that were not fellows.

I cast my eyes to the stranded vessel—when the breach and froth of the sea being so big I could hardly see it, it lay so far off—and considered, Lord! How was it possible I could get on shore?

Then I began to look around me to see what kind of a place I was in and what was next to be done; and I soon found that I had a dreadful deliverance, for I was wet, had no clothes to shift me, nor anything either to eat or drink to comfort me; neither did I see any prospect before me but that of perishing with hunger or being devoured by wild beasts: and that which was particularly afflicting to me was that I had no weapon either to hunt and kill any creature for my sustenance, or to defend myself against any other creature that might desire to kill me for theirs. In a word, I had nothing about me but a knife, a tobacco pipe, and a little tobacco in a box. This threw me into such terrible agonies of mind that, for a while, I ran about like a madman. Night coming upon me, I began, with a heavy heart, to consider what would be my lot if there were any ravenous beasts in that country, seeing at night they always come abroad for their prey.

All the remedy that offered to my thoughts was to get

up into a thick bushy tree, like a fir, but thorny—which grew near me, and where I resolved to sit all night—and consider the next day what death I should die, for I saw no prospect of life. I walked about a furlong from the shore to see if I could find any fresh water to drink, which I did, to my great joy; and having drunk and put a little tobacco into my mouth to prevent hunger, I went to the tree and, getting up into it, endeavored to place myself so as that, if I should fall asleep, I might not fall; and having cut a short stick, like a truncheon, for my defense, I took up my lodging; and being excessively fatigued, I fell asleep, and slept as comfortably as, I believe, few could have done in my condition.

⊰⊱ CHAPTER 4 ⊱⊰

WHEN I waked it was broad day, the weather clear and the storm abated, so that the sea did not rage and swell as before; but that which surprised me most was that the ship was lifted off in the night from the sand where she lay, by the swelling of the tide, and was driven up almost as far as the rock where I had been so bruised by the wave dashing me against it. This being within about a mile from the shore where I was, and the ship seeming to stand upright still, I wished myself on board, that I might save some necessary things for my use.

When I came down from my apartment in the tree, I looked about me again, and the first thing I found was the boat, which lay as the sea had tossed her up, upon the land, about two miles on my right hand. I walked as far as I could to get to her, but found a neck, or inlet, of water between me and the boat, which was about half a mile broad;

so I came back for the present, being more intent upon getting at the ship.

A little after noon, I found the sea very calm, and the tide ebbed so far out that I could come within a quarter of a mile of the ship: I pulled off most of my clothes, for the weather was hot to extremity, and took to the water; but when I came to the ship, my difficulty was still greater to know how to get on board; for, as she lay aground and high out of the water, there was nothing within my reach to lay hold of. I swam round her twice, and the second time I spied a small piece of rope hanging down by the forechains, and by the help of that rope got into the fore-castle. Here I found that the ship had a great deal of water in her hold; but that she lay so on the side of a bank of hard earth that all her quarter was free, and the ship's provisions were dry; and, being very well disposed to eat, I went to the bread room and filled my pockets with biscuit and ate it as I went about other things, for I had no time to lose. I also found some rum in the great cabin, of which I took a large dram to spirit me for what was before me. Now I wanted nothing but a boat, to furnish myself with many things which I foresaw would be very necessary to me.

It was in vain to sit still and wish for what was not to be had, and this extremity roused my application. We had several spare yards, and two or three large spars of wood, and a spare topmast or two in the ship; I flung as many overboard as I could manage for their weight, tying every one with a rope that they might not drive away. When this was done, I went down the ship's side, and pulling them to me, I tied four of them fast together at both ends in the form of a raft, and laying two or three short pieces of plank upon them crossways, I found I could walk upon it very well, but that it was not able to bear any great weight; so, with the carpenter's saw, I cut a spare topmast into three lengths, and added them to my raft, with a great deal of labor and pains.

My raft was now strong enough to bear any reasonable weight. I next laid all the boards upon it that I could get, and then I got three of the seamen's chests, which I had broken open and emptied, and lowered them down upon my raft; these I filled with provisions, viz., bread, rice, three Dutch cheeses, five pieces of dried goats' flesh, and a little remainder of European grain, which had been laid by for some fowls which we had brought to sea with us, but the fowls were killed. I found several cases of cordials and six gallons of rack. These I stowed by themselves, there being no room for them in the chests. While I was doing this, I found the tide began to foxy, though very calm; and I had the mortification to see my coat, shirt, and waistcoat, which I had left on shore, swim away; as for my breeches, which were only linen and open-kneed, I had them on, and my stockings. However, this put me upon rummaging for clothes, of which I took no more than I wanted for present use, for I had other things which my eye was more upon. After long searching, I found the carpenter's chest, which was much more valuable to me than a ship-lading of gold would have been at that time, and I got it down to my raft.

My next care was for some ammunition and arms. There were two very good fowling pieces in the great cabin, and two pistols; these I secured first, with some powder horns and a small bag of shot and two old rusty swords. I found three barrels of powder, two of them dry; the third had taken water. Those two I got to my raft, with the arms. And now I began to think how I should get to shore with my freight, having neither sail, oar, nor rudder; and the least capful of wind would have overset all my navigation.

I had three encouragements: first, a smooth, calm sea; secondly, the tide rising and setting in to the shore; thirdly, what little wind there was blew me towards the land. Thus, having found three broken oars, I put to sea. For a mile, or thereabouts, my raft went well, only that I found it drive a little distant from the place where I had landed before, by which I perceived that there was some indraft of the water, and consequently I hoped to find some creek or river there, which I might make use of as a port.

As I imagined, so it was: there appeared before me a little opening of the land and I found a strong current of the tide set into it; so I guided my raft into the middle of the stream. But here I had like to have suffered a second shipwreck, which, if I had, I think it verily would have broken my heart; for my raft ran aground at one end upon a shoal, and, not being aground at the other end, it wanted but a little that all my cargo had slipped off into the water. I did my utmost, by setting my back against the chests, to keep them in their places, but could not thrust off the raft with all my strength; neither durst I stir from the posture I was in, but holding up the chests with all my might, I stood in that manner near half an hour, in which time the rising of the water brought me a little more upon a level; and a little after, the water still rising, my raft floated again, and I thrust her off with the oar I had into the channel, and then, driving up higher, I at length found myself in the mouth of a little river, with a strong current or tide running up. I looked on both sides for a proper place to get to shore, for I was not willing to be driven too high up the river, hoping, in time, to see some ship at sea, and therefore resolved to place myself as near the coast as I could.

At length I spied a little cove on the right shore of the creek, to which, with great pain and difficulty, I guided my raft, and at last got so near as that, reaching ground with my oar, I could thrust her directly in; but here that shore lay so steep there was no place to land, but where one end of my float, if it ran on shore, would lie so high, and the other sink lower, as before, that I had like to have dipped all my cargo into the sea again. All that I could do was to wait till the tide was at the highest, keeping the raft with my oar like an anchor, to hold the side of it fast to the shore near a flat piece of ground, which I expected the water would flow over; and so it did. As soon as I found water enough, for my raft drew about a foot of water, I thrust her upon that flat piece of ground, and there moored her, by sticking my two broken oars into the ground, one on one side near one end, and one on the other side near the other end; and thus I lay till the water ebbed away and left my raft and all my cargo safe on shore.

Where I was I yet knew not; whether on the continent or on an island; whether inhabited or not inhabited; whether in danger of wild beasts or not. There was a hill not above a mile from me, which rose up very steep and high. I took out one of the fowling pieces and one of the pistols and a horn of powder; and thus armed, I traveled for discovery up to the top of that hill, where, after I had with great labor and difficulty got up to the top, I saw my fate, to my great affliction, viz., that I was in an island, environed every way with the sea, no land to be seen, except two smaller islands, which lay about three leagues to the west.

I found also that the island I was in was barren and, as I saw good reason to believe, uninhabited except by wild beasts, of whom, however, I saw none. At my coming back, I shot at a great bird which I saw sitting upon a tree on the side of a wood. I believe it was the first gun that had been fired there since the creation of the world; I had no sooner fired but from all the parts of the wood there arose an innumerable number of fowls of many sorts, making a confused screaming and crying, but not one of them of any kind that I knew. As for the creature I killed, I took it to be a kind of a hawk. Its flesh was carrion and fit for nothing.

I came back to my raft and fell to work to bring my cargo on shore, which took me up the rest of that day. I then barricaded myself round with the chests and boards that I had brought on shore and made a kind of hut for that night's lodging.

As I knew the first storm that blew must necessarily break the ship all in pieces, I resolved to set all other things apart till I got everything out of her that I could. Then I called a council, that is to say, in my thoughts, whether I should take back the raft; but this appeared impracticable; so I resolved to go as before, when the tide was down; and I did so.

I got on board the ship as before and prepared a second raft; and having had experience of the first, I neither made this so unwieldy nor loaded it so hard, but yet I brought away several things very useful to me. In the carpenter's stores, I found three bags of nails, a great screw jack, two dozen hatchets; and, above all, that most useful thing called a grindstone. All these I secured together with three iron crows and two barrels of musket bullets, seven muskets, another fowling piece, some small quantity of powder more, a large bag full of small shot. I took all the men's clothes that I could find, and a spare fore-topsail, a hammock, and some bedding; and with this I loaded my second raft and brought them all safe on shore, to my very great comfort.

I was under some apprehensions lest, during my absence from the land, my provisions might be devoured on shore. But when I came back, I found no sign of any visitor; only there sat a creature like a wildcat upon one of the chests, which, when I came towards it, ran away a little distance and then stood still. Very composed and unconcerned, she looked full in my face, as if she had a mind to be acquainted with me. I presented my gun to her, but as she did not understand it, she did not offer to stir away; upon which I tossed her a bit of biscuit, though I was not very free of it, for my store was not great; she went to it, smelled of it, and ate it, and looked for more; but I thanked her, and could spare no more, so she marched off.

Having got my second cargo on shore, I went to work to make me a little tent with the sail and some poles, which I cut for that purpose; and into this tent I brought everything that I knew would spoil either with rain or sun; and I piled all the empty chests and casks up in a circle round the tent to fortify it from any sudden attempt either from man or beast. I then blocked up the door of the tent with some boards within, and an empty chest set up on end without; and spreading my bedding upon the ground, laying my two pistols at my head and my gun at length by me, I went to bed and slept quietly all night, for I was very weary.

I had the biggest magazine of all kinds now that ever was laid up, I believe, for one man; but I was not satisfied still; for, while the ship sat upright in that posture, I thought I ought to get everything out of her that I could; so every day, at low water, I went on board and brought away something; but particularly the third time I went, I brought away as much of the rigging as I could, as also small ropes and rope twine, and the barrel of wet gunpowder. I cut the sails in pieces and brought as much each time as I could, for they were useful as canvas. But that which comforted me still more was that I found a great hogshead of bread, and three large runlets of rum or spirits, and a box of sugar, and a barrel of fine flour; I got all this safe on shore also.

The next day I made another voyage, and I began on the cables. Cutting the great cable into pieces I could move, I got two cables and a hawser on shore, with all the ironwork I could get; and having cut down the spritsail yard, and the mizzen yard, and everything I could to make a large raft, I loaded it with all those heavy goods and came away; but this raft was so unwieldy and so overladen that after I was entered the little cove, where I had landed the rest of my goods, not being able to guide it so handily as I did the other, it overset and threw me and all my cargo into the water; as for myself, it was no great harm, for I was near the shore; but as to my cargo, it was a great part of it lost, especially the iron; however, when the tide was out, I got most of the pieces of cable ashore, and some of the iron, though with infinite labor, for I was fain to dip for it into the water.

I had been now thirteen days ashore and had been eleven times on board the ship, in which time I had brought away all that one pair of hands could well be supposed capable to bring; though I believe verily, had the calm weather held, I should have brought away the whole ship piece by piece; but preparing, the twelfth time, to go on board, I found the wind began to rise. However, at low water I went on board; and though I thought I had rummaged the cabin so effectually as that nothing could be found, yet I discovered a locker with drawers in it, in one of which I found three razors and one pair of large scissors, with a dozen good knives and forks; in another I found about thirty-six pounds in money, some European coin, some Brazil, some pieces of eight, some gold, some silver.

I smiled to myself at the sight of this money. "O drug!" I exclaimed. "What art thou good for? Thou art not worth to me, no, not the taking off the ground; one of those knives is worth all this heap." However, upon second thoughts, I took it away; and while wrapping all this in a piece of canvas, I began to think of making another raft; but while I was preparing this, I found the sky overcast, and the wind began to rise, and in a quarter of an hour it blew a fresh gale from the shore. It occurred to me that it was in vain to make a raft with the wind offshore, and that it was my business to be gone before the tide of flood began. Accordingly I swam across the channel which lay between the ship and the sands, and even that with difficulty, partly with the weight of the things I had about me and partly the roughness of the water, for the wind rose very hastily and soon blew a storm.

I got home to my little tent, where I lay with all my wealth about me very secure. It blew very hard all that night, and in the morning, when I looked out, behold no more ship was to be seen! I was a little surprised, but recovered myself with this satisfactory reflection, viz., that I had lost no time, nor abated no diligence, to get everything out of her that could be useful to me.

My thoughts were now wholly employed about securing myself against savages, if any should appear, or wild beasts, if any were on the island; and about what kind of dwelling to make, whether a cave in the earth or a tent upon the earth; and, in short, I resolved upon both, the manner and description of which it may not be improper to give an account of.

The place I was in was upon a low, moorish ground near the sea, and I believed it would not be wholesome; and more particularly there was no fresh water near it, so I resolved to find a more healthy and more convenient spot of ground. I consulted several things in my situation, which I found would be proper for me: first, air and fresh water; secondly, shelter from the heat of the sun; thirdly, security from ravenous creatures, whether men or beasts; fourthly, a view to the sea, that if God sent any ship in sight, I might not lose any advantage for my deliverance.

In search for a place proper for this, I found a little plain on the side of a rising hill, whose front towards this little plain was steep as a house side, so that nothing could come down upon me from the top. On the side of this rock, there was a hollow place, worn a little way in like the entrance of a cave; but there was not really any cave. On the flat of the green, just before this hollow place, I resolved to pitch my tent. This plain was not above a hundred yards broad, and about twice as long, and lay like a green before my door; and, at the end, descended irregularly down into the low ground by the seaside. It was on the north-northwest side of the hill, so that it was sheltered from the heat.

I drew a half circle before the hollow place, which took in about ten yards in its radius from the rock, and twenty yards in its diameter, from its beginning and ending. In this half circle I pitched two rows of strong stakes, driving them into the ground till they stood very firm like piles, the biggest end being out of the ground about five feet and a half and sharpened on the top. The two rows did not stand above six inches from one another.

Then I took the pieces of cable which I cut in the ship, and laid them in rows, one upon another, within the circle; between these two rows of stakes, up to the top, placing other stakes in the inside, leaning against them, about two feet and a half high, like a spur to a post; and this fence was so strong that neither man nor beast could get into it or over it. This cost me a great deal of time and labor, especially to cut the piles in the woods, bring them to the place, and drive them into the earth.

The entrance into this place I made to be not by a door, but by a short ladder to go over the top; which ladder, when I was in, I lifted over after me, and so I was completely fenced in and fortified, as I thought, from all the world, and consequently slept secure in the night, which otherwise I could not have done.

⊰꙳ CHAPTER 5 ꙳⊱

INTO this fence or fortress, with infinite labor, I carried all my riches, my provisions, ammunition, and stores; and I made a large tent, which, to preserve me from the rains, that in one part of the year are very violent there, I made double, viz., one smaller tent within and one larger tent above it, and covered the uppermost with a large tarpaulin, which I had saved among the sails. Into this tent I brought all my provisions; and I made up the entrance, which till now I had left open, and so passed and repassed as I said, by a short ladder. And now I lay in a hammock, which was indeed a good one and belonged to the mate of the ship.

When I had done this, I began to work my way into the rock, and bringing all the earth and stones that I dug down out through my tent, I laid them up within my fence in the nature of a terrace so that it raised the ground within about a foot and a half; and thus I made me a cave, just behind my tent, which served me like a cellar to my house. It cost me much labor and many days before these things were brought to perfection, and therefore I must go back to some other things which took up some of my thoughts. It happened, after I had laid my scheme for the setting up my tent, that a storm of rain falling from a thick, dark cloud, a sudden flash of lightning happened, and after that, a great clap of thunder. I was not so much surprised with the lightning as I was with a thought which darted into my mind as swift as the lightning itself: O my powder! My heart sunk within me when I thought that at one blast all my powder might be destroyed; on which both my defense and the providing me food depended. I was nothing near so anxious about my own danger, though, had the powder taken fire, I should never have known what had hurt me.

Such impression did this make upon me, that after the storm was over, I laid aside all my building and fortifying, and applied myself to make bags and boxes to separate the powder and to keep it a little and a little in a parcel, in hope that, whatever might come, it might not be possible to make one part fire another. I finished this work in about a fortnight; and I think my powder, which in all was about two hundred and forty pounds' weight, was divided into not less than a hundred parcels. As to the barrel that had been wet, I did not apprehend any danger from that; so I placed it in my new cave, which, in my fancy, I called my kitchen, and the rest I had up and down in holes among the rocks so that no wet might come to it, marking carefully where I laid it.

While this was doing, I went out at least once every day with my gun as well to divert myself as to see if I could kill anything fit for food; and, as near as I could, to acquaint myself with what the island produced. The first time I went out, I discovered that there were goats upon the island, but they were so shy, so subtle, and so swift of foot that it was most difficult to come at them; but I was not discouraged at this; for, after I had found their haunts a little, I laid wait in this manner for them: I observed, if they saw me in the valleys, though they were upon the rocks, they would run away; but if they were feeding in the valleys, and I was upon the rocks, they took no notice of me; from whence I concluded that they did not readily see objects that were above them. So afterwards I climbed the rocks to get above them and then had frequently a fair mark. The first shot I made among these creatures, I killed a she-goat, which had a little kid by her, which she gave suck to, which grieved me heartily; but when the old one fell, the kid stood stock-still by her till I came and took her up; and when I carried the old one with me upon my shoulders, the kid followed me quite to my enclosure, upon which I laid down the dam and took the kid in my arms and carried it over my pale, in hopes to have bred it up tame: but it would not eat, so I was forced to kill it and eat it myself. These two supplied me with flesh a great while, for I ate sparingly and preserved my provisions (my bread especially) as much as possibly I could.

I MUST now give some little account of myself and of my thoughts about living, which, it may well be supposed, were not a few. I had a dismal prospect of my condition; for, as I was not cast away upon that island without being driven by a violent storm some hundreds of leagues out of the ordinary course of the trade of mankind, I had great reason to consider it as a determination of Heaven, that in this desolate place, and in this desolate manner, I should end my life. The tears would run plentifully down my face when I made these reflections, and sometimes I would expostulate with myself why Providence should thus completely ruin its creatures.

But something always returned swift upon me to check these thoughts and to reprove me; and then it occurred to me how well I was furnished, and what would have been my case if it had not happened (which was a hundred thousand to one) that the ship floated from the place where she first struck, and was driven so near to shore that I had time to get all these things out of her; what would have been my case if I had had to live in the condition in which I at first came on shore, without the necessaries of life?

After I had been upon this island about ten days, it came to my thoughts that I should lose my reckoning of time and should even forget the Sabbath days from the working days; but, to prevent this, I cut it with my knife upon a large post, in capital letters; and making it into a great cross, I set it up on the shore where I first landed, viz., I CAME ON SHORE HERE ON THE 30TH OF SEPTEMBER, 1659. Upon the sides of this square post I cut every day a notch with my knife, and every seventh notch was as long again as the rest, and every first day of the month as long again as that long one; and thus I kept my calendar.

I found sometime after, in rummaging the chests, several things most useful to me, as pens, ink and paper; several parcels in the captain's keeping; three compasses, some mathematical instruments, dials, charts and books of navigation, all of which I huddled together, whether I might want them or no; also I found three very good Bibles, prayerbooks and several other books. And I must not forget that we had in the ship a dog and two cats. I carried both the cats with me; and as for the dog, he jumped out of the ship himself and swam on shore to me the day after I went on shore with my first cargo and was a trusty servant to me for many years; I wanted nothing that he could fetch me, nor any company that he could make up to me. I only wanted to have him talk to me, but that he would not do.

Notwithstanding all that I had amassed, I wanted many things, as a spade, pickaxe and shovel, to dig or remove the earth; needles, pins and thread. This want of tools made every work I did go on heavily, and it was near a whole year before I had finished my habitation. The stakes, which were as heavy as I could well lift, were a long time in cutting and preparing in the woods, and more, by far, in bringing home;

so that I spent sometimes two days in cutting and bringing home one post, and a third day in driving it into the ground. But why be concerned at the tediousness of anything I had to do, seeing I had time enough to do it in?

I now began to consider seriously the circumstance I was reduced to; and I drew up the state of my affairs in writing, not so much to leave them to any that were to come after me (for I was like to have but few heirs) as to deliver my thoughts from daily poring upon them and afflicting my mind; and as my reason began now to master my despondency, I began to comfort myself as well as I could, and to set the good against the evil, that I might have something to distinguish my case from worse. And I stated very impartially, like debtor and creditor, the comforts I enjoyed against the miseries I suffered, thus:

EVIL	GOOD
I am cast upon a horrible, desolate island, void of all hope of recovery.	But I am alive; and not drowned, as all my ship's company were.
I am singled out and separated, as it were, from all the world, to be miserable.	But I am singled out too from all the ship's crew, to be spared from death; and He that miraculously saved me from death can deliver me from this condition.
I am divided from mankind, a solitaire; one banished from human society.	But I am not starved, and perishing in a barren place, affording no sustenance.

I am without any defense or means to resist any violence of man or beast.	But I am cast on an island where I see no wild beast to hurt me, as I saw on the coast of Africa; and what if I had been shipwrecked there?
I have no soul to speak to or relieve me.	But God wonderfully sent the ship in near enough to the shore, that I have got out so many necessary things as will either supply my wants or enable me to supply myself, even as long as I live.

Upon the whole, here was an undoubted testimony that there was scarce any condition in the world so miserable, but there was something negative, or something positive, to be thankful for in it.

Having now brought my mind a little to relish my condition, and given over looking out to sea, to see if I could spy a ship, I began to apply myself to make things as easy to me as I could.

Against my fence I raised a wall of turfs, about two feet thick on the outside; and after some time (I think it was a year and a half) I raised rafters from it, leaning to the rock, and covered it with boughs of trees, and such things as I could get, to keep out the rain, which I found at some times of the year very violent.

I had brought all my goods into this pale, and into the cave which I had made behind me. But at first this was a confused heap of goods, which took up all my place. I had no room to turn myself, so I set myself to enlarge my cave and work farther into the earth; for it was a loose sandy rock, which yielded easily to the labor I bestowed on it. I worked sideways, to the right hand, into the rock and then, turning to the right again, worked quite out and made me a door to come out in the outside of my fortification. This gave me not only a back way to my tent and to my store house but gave me room to stow my goods.

And now I began to apply myself to make a chair and a table, for without these I was not able to enjoy the few comforts I had in the world; I could not write, or eat, or do several things with so much pleasure, without a table. And here I must needs observe that, as reason is the substance and original of the mathematics, so, by stating and squaring everything by reason, and by making the most rational judgment of things, every man may be, in time, master of every mechanic art. I had never handled a tool in my life; and yet, in time, by labor, application and contrivance I found at last that I wanted nothing but I could have made, especially if I had had the proper tools. However, I made abundance of things with no more tools than an adze and a hatchet, which perhaps were never made that way before, and that with infinite labor. For example, if I wanted a board, I had no other way but to cut down a tree, set it on an edge before me, and hew it flat on either side with my axe till I had brought it to be as thin as a plank, and then dub it smooth with my adze. By this method, I could make but one board of a whole tree; but my time or labor was little worth, and so it was as well employed one way as another.

I made me a table and a chair out of the boards that I brought on my raft from the ship. I made shelves, one over another, all along one side of my cave, to lay all my tools, nails and ironwork on and to separate everything in their places that I might easily come at them. I knocked pieces into the wall of the rock to hang my guns and all things that would hang up, so that my cave looked like a magazine of all necessary things; and it was a great pleasure to me to see all my goods in such order and especially to find my stock of all necessaries so great.

And now, having settled my habitation, made me a table and a chair, and all as handsome about me as I could, I began to keep a journal, of which I shall here give you the copy (though in it will be told some of these particulars over again) as long as it lasted; for, having in the end no more ink, I was forced to leave it off.

⊰〉| CHAPTER 6 |〈⊱

OCTOBER 25. It rained all night and all day, with some gusts of wind, during which time the ship broke in pieces and was no more to be seen, except the wreck of her, and that only at low water. I spent this day in covering and securing the goods which I had saved, that the rain might not spoil them.

NOVEMBER 5. This day went abroad with my gun and dog, and killed a wildcat; her skin pretty soft, but her flesh good for nothing. I took off the skin and preserved it. Coming back by the shore, I saw many sorts of seafowl which I did not understand; but was surprised, and almost frightened, with two seals, which while I was gazing at them got into the sea and escaped me.

NOV. 17. This day I began to dig behind my tent, into the rock, to make room for my farther convenience.

Note. Three things I wanted exceedingly for this work,

viz., a pickaxe, a shovel, and a wheelbarrow or basket; so I desisted from my work and began to consider how to supply these wants. As for a pickaxe, I made use of the iron crows, which were proper enough, though heavy; but the next thing was a shovel, which was absolutely necessary; but what kind of one to make I knew not.

Nov. 18. The next day, in searching the woods, I found a tree of that wood, or like it, which in the Brazils they call the iron tree, from its exceeding hardness; of this, with great labor, and almost spoiling my axe, I cut a piece and brought it home, too, with difficulty enough, for it was exceeding heavy. I worked it effectually, by little and little, into the form of a shovel or spade; the handle exactly shaped like ours in England, only that the broad part having no iron shod upon it at bottom, it would not last me so long; however, it served well enough for the uses which I had occasion to put it to; but never was a shovel, I believe, made after that fashion or so long in making.

A basket I could not make by any means, having no such things as twigs that would bend to make wickerware; and as to the wheelbarrow, I fancied I could make all but the wheel, but that I had no notion how to go about. Besides, I had no way to make iron gudgeons for the spindle or axis of the wheel to run in, so for carrying away the earth which I dug out of the cave, I made me a thing like a hod, which the laborers carry mortar in for the bricklayers. This was not so difficult as making the shovel, and yet this and the shovel and the vain attempt to make a wheelbarrow took me no less than four days; I mean, always excepting my morning walk with my gun, which I seldom omitted, and very seldom failed also bringing home something fit to eat.

NOV. 23. My other work having stood still because of my making these tools, I now spent eighteen days in widening and deepening my cave.

DECEMBER 10. I began to think my cave or vault finished, when on a sudden (it seems I had made it too large) a great quantity of earth fell down from the top and one side, so much that it frightened me, and not without reason too; for, if I had been under it, I should never have wanted a gravedigger. Upon this disaster, I had a great deal of work to do over again, for I had the loose earth to carry out; and, which was of more importance, I had the ceiling to prop up so that I might be sure no more would come down.

DEC. 11. This day I got two posts pitched upright to the top, with two pieces of board across over each post; this I finished the next day, and setting more posts up with boards, in about a week more I had the roof secured; and the posts, standing in rows, served me for partitions to part off my house.

DEC. 17. From this day to the 30th I placed shelves, and knocked up nails on the posts, to hang everything up that could be hung up.

DEC. 24. Much rain all night and all day; no stirring out.

DEC. 25. Rain all day.

DEC. 26. No rain; earth cooler than before and pleasanter.

DEC. 27. Killed a young goat and lamed another, so that I catched it and led it home in a string; when I had it home, I bound and splintered up its leg, which was broke.

N.B. I took such care of it that it lived, and the leg grew as strong as ever; but by nursing it so long, it grew tame, and fed upon the little green at my door and would not go away. This revived a thought of breeding up some tame creatures that I might have food when my powder and shot was all spent.

DEC. 28, 29, 30, 31. Great heats and no breeze, so that there was no stirring abroad, except in the evening, for food; this time I spent in putting all my things in order within doors.

JANUARY 1. Very hot still; but I went abroad early and late with my gun, and lay still in the middle of the day. This evening, going farther into the valleys which lay towards the center of the island, I found there was plenty of goats, though exceeding shy and hard to come at; however, I resolved to try if I could not bring my dog to hunt them down. Accordingly, the next day, I went out with my dog and set him upon the goats; but I was mistaken, for they all faced about upon the dog; and he knew his danger too well, for he would not come near them.

JAN. 3. I began my wall, which, being still jealous of my

being attacked by somebody, I resolved to make very thick and strong.

N.B. I was no less time than from the 3rd of January to the 14th of April working, finishing and perfecting this wall; though it was no more than twenty-five yards in length, being a half circle, from one place in the rock to another place, the door of the cave being in the center, behind it. All this time I worked very hard, the rains hindering me many days, nay, sometimes weeks together. But when this wall was finished, with a turf wall raised up close to the outside, I persuaded myself that if any people were to come on shore there, they would not perceive anything like a habitation; and it was very well I did so, as may be observed hereafter.

DURING this time I made my rounds in the woods for game every day, when the rain permitted me, and made frequent discoveries in these walks of something or other to my advantage; particularly, I found a kind of wild pigeons, who build, not as wood pigeons, in a tree, but rather as house pigeons, in the holes of the rocks; and taking some young ones, I endeavored to breed them up tame and did so. But when they grew older, they flew all away, which, perhaps, was for want of feeding them, for I had nothing to give them; however, I frequently found their nests and got their young ones, which were very good meat.

And now, in managing my household affairs, I found

myself wanting in many things, which I thought at first it was impossible for me to make; as indeed, as to some of them, it was: for instance, I could never make a cask to be hooped, though I spent many weeks about it; I could neither put in the heads nor join the staves so true to one another as to make them hold water, so I gave that also over. In the next place, I was at a great loss for candles; so that as soon as it was dark, which was generally by seven o'clock, I was obliged to go to bed. The only remedy I had was that when I had killed a goat, I saved the tallow, and with a little dish made of clay, which I baked in the sun, to which I added a wick of some oakum, I made me a lamp; and this gave me light, though not a clear steady light like a candle. In the middle of all my labors it happened that, in rummaging my things, I found a little bag, which, as I hinted before, had been filled with grain, for the feeding of poultry on board ship. What little grain remained appeared to be devoured by the rats, and I saw nothing in the bag but husks and dust; and being willing to have the bag for some other use (I think it was to put powder in), I shook the husks out of it on one side of my fortification under the rock.

About a month after, I saw some few stalks of something green shooting out of the ground, and not remembering that I had thrown anything there, I fancied this was some plant I had not seen; but I was surprised when, after a little longer time, I saw ten or twelve ears come out, which were perfect green English barley.

It is impossible to express the astonishment and confusion of my thoughts on this occasion. I had hitherto acted upon no religious foundation at all; indeed, I had very few notions of religion in my head. But after I saw barley grow there, in a climate which I knew was not proper for grain, and especially as I remembered not how it came there, it startled me strangely; and I began to suggest that God had miraculously caused this grain to grow without any help of seed sown, and that it was so directed purely for my sustenance on that wild miserable place.

This touched my heart a little and brought tears out of my eyes; and I began to bless myself that such a prodigy of nature should happen upon my account; and this was the more strange to me, because I saw near it, all along by the side of the rock, some other straggling stalks, which proved to be stalks of rice.

I not only thought these the pure productions of Providence for my support, but, not doubting that there was more in the place, I went over all that part of the island where I had been before, searching in every corner and under every rock; but I could not find any. At last it occurred to my thoughts that I had shook out a bag of chicken's grain in that place, and then the wonder began to cease; and I must confess, my religious thankfulness to God's providence began to abate too, upon the discovering that all this was nothing but what was common; though I ought to have been thankful, for it was really the work of Providence that ten or twelve seeds should remain unspoiled when the rats had destroyed all the rest; as also, that I should throw it out in that particular place, where, it being in the shade of a high rock, it sprang up immediately; whereas, if I had thrown it anywhere else at that time, it would have been burned up by the sun.

I carefully saved the ears of this grain, you may be sure, in their season, which was about the end of June; and, laying up every seed of barley and rice, I resolved to sow them all again, hoping, in time, to have some quantity sufficient to supply me with bread. But it was not till the fourth year that I could allow myself the least grain to eat, and even then but sparingly, as I shall show afterwards in its order. But to return to my journal.

APRIL 22. I was at a great loss about my tools, which, with much chopping and cutting knotty hard wood, were all full of notches and dull; and, though I had a grindstone, I could not turn it and grind my tools too. This caused me as much thought as a statesman would have bestowed upon a grand point of politics, or a judge upon the life and death of a man. At length I contrived a wheel with a string, to turn it with my foot, that I might have both my hands at liberty.

Note. I had never seen any such thing in England, or at least not to take notice how it was done, though since I have observed it is very common there. This machine cost me a full week's work to bring it to perfection.

APRIL 28, 29. These two whole days I took up in grinding my tools, my machine for turning my grindstone per-forming very well.

APRIL 30. Having perceived that my bread had been low a great while, I now took a survey of it and reduced myself to one biscuit a day, which made my heart very heavy.

❧ CHAPTER 7 ❧

MAY 1. In the morning, looking towards the seaside, the tide being low, I saw something lie on the shore bigger than ordinary, and it looked like a cask; when I came to it, I found a small barrel and two or three pieces of the wreck of the ship, which were driven on shore by a severe storm; and, looking towards the wreck itself, I thought it seemed to lie higher out of the water than it used to do. I examined the barrel and found it was a barrel of gunpowder; but it had taken water, and the powder was caked as hard as stone. I rolled it farther on the shore for the present and went on upon the sands as near as I could to the wreck of the ship.

When I came down to the ship, I found it strangely removed. The sand was thrown so high on the side next her stern that I could now walk quite up to her when the tide was out; whereas there was a great piece of water before, so that I could not come within a quarter of a mile of the wreck without swimming. I was surprised with this at first, but soon concluded it must be done by the storm. The ship was more broken open than formerly, so many things came daily on shore which the sea had loosened, and which the winds and water rolled by degrees to the land.

I busied myself mightily in searching whether I could make any way into the ship, but I found all the inside of her was choked up with sand. However, as I had learned not to despair of anything, I resolved to pull everything to pieces that I could of the ship, concluding that everything I could get from her would be of some use or other to me.

MAY 3. I began with my saw and cut a piece of a beam through, which I thought held some of the upper part or quarterdeck together; and when I had cut it through, I cleared away the sand as well as I could from the side which lay highest; but the tide coming in, I was obliged to give over for that time.

MAY 4. I went a-fishing, but caught not one fish that I durst eat of, till I was weary of my sport; when, just going to leave off, I caught a young dolphin. I had made me a long line of some rope yarn, but I had no hooks; yet I frequently caught fish enough; all which I dried in the sun and ate them dry.

MAY 5. Worked on the wreck: cut another beam asunder and brought three great fir planks off from the decks, which I tied together, and made swim on shore when the tide of flood came on.

MAY 6. Worked on the wreck: got several iron bolts out of her and other pieces of ironwork; worked very hard, and came home very much tired, and had thoughts of giving it over.

MAY 7. Went to the wreck again but found the weight of the wreck had broke itself down, the beams being cut; that several pieces of the ship seemed to lie loose, and the inside of the hold lay so open that I could see into it, but almost full of water and sand.

MAY 8 to 14. Went every day to the wreck and got a great many pieces of timber, and two or three hundred-weight of iron.

MAY 15 to JUNE 15. I continued to work every day on the wreck, except the time necessary to get food, which I always appointed to be when the tide was up, that I might be ready when it was ebbed out; and by this time I had gotten timber, and plank, and ironwork, enough to have built a good boat if I had known how, and I got near one hundredweight of sheet lead.

JUNE 16. Going down to the seaside, I found a large tortoise, or turtle. This was the first I had seen, which, it seems, was only my misfortune, not any defect of the place or scarcity; for had I happened to be on the other side of the island, I might have had hundreds of them every day, as I found afterwards.

JUNE 17. I spent in cooking the turtle. I found in her threescore eggs; and her flesh was to me, at that time, the most savory and pleasant that I ever tasted in my life, having had no flesh, but of goats and fowls, since I landed in this horrid place.

JUNE 18. Rained all that day, and I stayed within. I thought, at this time, the rain felt cold, and I was somewhat chilly; which I knew was not usual in that latitude.

JUNE 19. Very ill, and shivering, as if the weather had been cold.

JUNE 20. No rest all night; violent pains in my head, and feverish.

JUNE 21. Very ill; frightened almost to death with the apprehensions of my sad condition, to be sick and no help; prayed to God for the first time since the storm off Hull; but scarce knew what I said, or why, my thoughts being all confused.

JUNE 22. A little better but under dreadful apprehensions of sickness.

JUNE 23. Very bad again, cold and shivering, and then a violent headache.

JUNE 24. Much better.

JUNE 25. A cold fit, and hot, with faint sweats after it.

JUNE 26. Better; and, having no victuals to eat, took my gun but found myself very weak; however, I killed a she-goat, and with much difficulty got it home, and broiled some of it, and ate. I would fain have stewed it, and made some broth, but had no pot.

JUNE 27. An ague so violent that I lay a-bed all day. I was ready to perish for thirst, but so weak I had not strength to stand up or to get myself any water to drink.

Prayed to God again, but was light-headed; and when I was not, I was so ignorant that I knew not what to say, only lay and cried, "Lord, look upon me! Lord, pity me! Lord, have mercy upon me!" I suppose I did nothing else for two or three hours till, the fit wearing off, I fell asleep, and did not wake till far in the night. When I awoke, I found myself much refreshed but weak and exceeding thirsty; however, as I had no water in my whole habitation, I was forced to lie till morning and went to sleep again. In this second sleep I had this terrible dream: I thought that I was sitting on the ground, on the outside of my wall, and that I saw a man descend from a great black cloud in a bright flame of fire, so that I could but just bear to look towards him. His countenance was too dreadful for words to describe. When he stepped upon the ground, I thought the earth trembled; and all the air looked as if it had been filled with flashes of fire. He had no sooner landed upon the earth but he moved towards me, with a long spear in his hand; and when he came to a rising ground, at some distance, he spoke to me in a voice so terrible that it is impossible to express the terror of it. All that I understood was: *Seeing all these things have not brought thee to repentance, now thou shalt die;* at which words, I thought he lifted up the spear that was in his hand to kill me.

No one that shall ever read this account will expect that I should be able to describe the horrors of my soul at this terrible vision; the impression that remained upon my mind when I awaked, and found it was but a dream. I had, alas, no divine knowledge; what I had received by the good instruction of my father was then worn out by eight years of seafaring wickedness and conversation with none but such as were, like myself, profane to the last degree. I was all that the most hardened, unthinking creature among our common sailors can be supposed to be; not having the least sense, either of the fear of God, in danger, or thankfulness to him, in deliverances.

It is true, when I first got on shore here and found all my ship's crew drowned and myself spared, I was surprised with a kind of ecstasy, and some transports of soul, which, had the grace of God assisted, might have come up to true thankfulness; but it ended where it began, in a mere common flight of joy or, as I may say, being glad I was alive, without the least reflection upon the distinguished goodness of the hand which had preserved me, and had singled me out to be preserved when all the rest were destroyed.

The growing up of the grain, as is hinted in my journal, had, at first, some little influence upon me and began to affect me with seriousness, as long as I thought it had something miraculous in it; but as soon as that part of the thought was removed, all the impression which was raised from it wore off also, as I have noted already. But now, when I began to be sick and a leisure view of the miseries of death came to place itself before me, when my spirits began to sink under the burden of a strong distemper and nature was exhausted with the violence of the fever, conscience, that had slept so long, began to awake, and I said aloud, "My dear father's words are come to pass: God's justice has overtaken me." Then I cried out, "Lord, be my help, for I am in great distress." This was the first prayer, if I may call it so, that I had made for many years— But I return to my journal.

JUNE 28. Having been somewhat refreshed with the sleep I had had, and the fit being entirely off, I got up; and though the terror of my dream was very great, yet I considered that the ague would return again the next day, and now was my time to get something to refresh and support myself when I should be ill. So I filled a large square case bottle with water and set it upon my table in reach of my bed; and to take off the aguish disposition of the water, I put about a quarter of a pint of rum into it and mixed them together. Then I got me a piece of the goat's flesh and broiled it on the coals, but could eat very little. I walked about but was very weak and, withal very sad, dreading the return of my distemper. At night, I made my supper of three turtle's eggs, which I roasted in the ashes and ate, as we call it, in the shell; and this was the first bit of meat I had ever asked God's blessing to, as I could remember, in my whole life.

After I had eaten, I tried to walk but found myself so weak that I could hardly carry the gun (for I never went out without that); so I went but a little way and sat down upon the ground, looking out upon the sea, which was just before me, and very calm and smooth. As I sat here, these thoughts occurred to me: What is this earth and sea, of which I have seen so much? And what am I, and all the other creatures, wild and tame? Surely, we are all made by some secret power who formed the earth and sea, the air and sky. And who is that? Then it followed most naturally, It is God. Well, but then the power that could make all things must certainly have power to guide and direct them; if so, nothing can happen in the great circuit of His works, without His knowledge or appointment. Therefore, He knows that I am here and in this dreadful condition, and He has appointed all this to befall me.

Immediately it followed, Why has God done this to me? What have I done to be thus used? My conscience presently checked me in that inquiry, as if I had blasphemed; and methought it spoke to me like a voice, Wretch! Dost *thou* ask what thou has done? Look back upon a dreadful misspent life, and ask thyself what thou hast *not* done? Ask, why is it that thou were not long ago destroyed? Why wert thou not drowned in Yarmouth Roads; killed in the fight when the ship was taken by the Sallee man-of-war; devoured by the wild beasts on the coast of Africa; or drowned *here,* when all the crew perished but thyself? I was struck dumb with these reflections and had no answer to myself; and, rising up pensive and sad, walked back to my retreat and went over my wall, as if I had been going to bed; but my thoughts were sadly disturbed, and I had no inclination to sleep; so I sat down in the chair and lighted my lamp, for it began to be dark.

Now, as the apprehension of the return of my distemper terrified me very much, it occurred to my thought that the Brazilians take no physic but their tobacco for almost all distempers, and I had some tobacco in one of the chests.

I was directed by Heaven, no doubt; for in this chest I found a cure both for soul and body. I opened the chest and found the tobacco; and as the few books I had saved lay there too, I took out one of the Bibles which, to this time, I had not found leisure or so much as inclination to look into. I brought that and the tobacco with me to the table. What use to make of the tobacco I knew not, as to my distemper; but I tried several experiments. I first took a piece and chewed it; which, at first, almost stupefied my brain, the tobacco being green and strong. Then I steeped some an hour or two in some rum and resolved to take a dose of it when I lay down; and lastly, I burned some upon a pan of coals and held my nose close over the smoke of it as long as I could bear it. In the interval of this operation I took up the Bible and began to read, but my head was too much disturbed by the tobacco to bear reading at that time; only, having opened the book casually, the first words that occurred to me were: *And call upon me in the day of trouble: I will deliver thee, and thou shalt glorify me.* These words were very apt to my case, and I mused upon them.

It now grew late, and the tobacco had dozed my head so much that I inclined to sleep; so I left my lamp burning in the cave, lest I should want anything in the night, and went to bed. But before I lay down, I did what I never had done in all my life: I kneeled down and prayed to God to fulfill the promise to me, that if I called upon Him in the day of trouble, He would deliver me. After my broken and imperfect prayer, I drank the rum in which I had steeped the tobacco, which was so strong and rank that I could scarce get it down; immediately upon this I went to bed. The rum flew up into my head violently; but I fell into a sound sleep and waked no more till, by the sun, it must be near three o'clock in the afternoon the next day; nay, to this hour, I am partly of opinion that I slept all the next day and night, and till almost three the day after; for otherwise, I know not how I should lose a day out of my reckoning in the days of the week, as it appeared, some years after, I had done. When I awaked, I found myself refreshed, and my spirits lively and cheerful; when I got up, I was stronger and my stomach better, for I was hungry. I had no fit the next day, but continued much altered for the better.

The 30th I went abroad with my gun, but did not travel far. I killed two seafowl and brought them home; but was not very forward to eat them, so I ate some more turtle's eggs, which were very good. This evening I renewed the medicine, which I had supposed did me good the day before, viz., the tobacco steeped in rum; only I did not take so much as before, nor did I chew any of the leaf or hold my head over the smoke; however, I was not so well the next day as I hoped I should have been.

JULY 2. I renewed the medicine all the three ways and dosed myself with it as at first.

JULY 3. I missed the fit for good and all, though I did not recover my full strength for some weeks after. While I was thus gathering strength, my thoughts ran exceedingly upon this Scripture, *I will deliver thee;* and the impossibility of my deliverance lay much upon my mind, in bar of my ever expecting it. But, as I was discouraging myself with such thoughts, it occurred to my mind that I pored so much upon my deliverance from the main affliction that I disregarded the deliverance I had received; and I was, as it were, made to ask myself such questions as these, viz., Has not God delivered me, and wonderfully, too, from sickness? And what notice have I taken of it? I have not glorified Him and been thankful. This touched my heart very much, and immediately I knelt down and gave God thanks aloud for my recovery.

JULY 4. In the morning I took the Bible, and beginning at the New Testament, I began seriously to read it and imposed upon myself to read awhile every morning and every night, not binding myself to the number of chapters, but as long as my thoughts should engage me. It was not long after I set seriously to this work that I found my heart more deeply and sincerely affected with the wickedness of my past life. The impression of my dream revived, and the words, *All these things have not brought thee to repentance,* ran seriously in my thoughts. I was earnestly begging of God to give me repentance, when it happened providen-

DANIEL DEFOE

tially, the very same day, that reading the Scripture, I came to these words: *Him hath God exalted with his right hand to be a Prince and a Saviour, for to give repentance to Israel, and forgiveness of sins.* I threw down the book, and with my heart as well as my hands lifted up to heaven in a kind of ecstasy of joy, I cried out aloud, "Jesus, thou son of David! Jesus, thou exalted Prince and Saviour, give me repentance!" I now prayed with a sense of my condition and with a true Scripture view of hope, founded on the encouragement of the word of God.

Now I began to construe the words, *Call upon me, I will deliver thee,* in a different sense from what I had ever done before; for then I had no notion of anything being called *deliverance* but my being delivered from my island prison. But now I learned to take it in another sense: I looked back upon my past life with such horror, and my sins appeared so dreadful, that my soul sought nothing of God but deliverance from the load of guilt that bore down all my comfort. As for my solitary life, it was nothing; I did not so much as pray to be delivered from it, or think of it.

❈| CHAPTER 8 |❈

I HAD now been in this unhappy island above ten months, and I firmly believed that no other human shape had ever set foot upon that place. Having secured my habitation, as I thought, I had a great desire to make a more perfect discovery of the island.

On the 15th of July I went up the creek, where I had brought my rafts on shore. I found, about two miles up, that the tide did not flow any higher, and that it was no more than a little brook of running water, very fresh and good; but, this being the dry season, there was hardly any water in some parts of it. On the banks of this brook I found many pleasant meadows, covered with grass; and on the higher parts of them, I found a great deal of tobacco, green, and growing to a very great and strong stalk. I saw large plants of aloes, but had no understanding about them. I saw several sugarcanes, but wild and, for want of

cultivation, imperfect. I contented myself with these discoveries for this time and came back, musing with myself
what course I might take to know the virtue of any of the
fruits or plants which I should discover.

The next day I went up the same way again; and after
going something farther, I found the country become more
woody than before. In this part I found different fruits;
and particularly I found melons upon the ground in great
abundance, and grapevines spread over the trees, and the
clusters of grapes were just in their prime, very ripe and
rich. This was a surprising discovery, and I was exceedingly
glad of them. I decided to cure them in the sun and keep
them as dried grapes or raisins are kept.

I spent all that evening there and went not back to my
habitation, which, by the way, was the first night, as I
might say, I had lain from home. At night, I took my first
contrivance and got up into a tree, where I slept well; and
the next morning proceeded on my discovery, traveling
near four miles, as I might judge by the length of the valley, keeping still due north, with a ridge of hills on the
south and north sides of me. At the end of this march I
came to an opening, where the country seemed to descend
to the west; and a little spring of fresh water issued out at
the side of a hill by me; and the country appeared so fresh,
so green, so flourishing that it looked like a planted garden. I descended a little on the side of that delicious vale,
surveying it with a secret kind of pleasure (though mixed
with other afflicting thoughts), to think that this was all

my own, that I was king and lord of all this country inde-
feasibly and had a right of possession; and, if I could convey it, I might have it in inheritance as completely as any
lord of a manor in England. I saw here abundance of co-
coa trees, and orange, lemon and lime trees; and the limes
that I gathered were not only pleasant to eat, but very
wholesome. I mixed their juice afterwards with water,
which made it cool and refreshing. I now resolved to lay
up a store of grapes, as well as limes and lemons, to furnish
myself for the wet season, which I knew was approaching.
I gathered a great heap of grapes in one place, and a great
parcel of limes and lemons in another place; and taking a
few of each with me, I traveled homeward and resolved to
come again and bring a bag or sack to carry the rest home.
Accordingly, having spent three days in this journey, I
came home (so I must now call my tent and my cave); but
before I got thither, the grapes were spoiled, the richness
of the fruits and the weight of the juice, having broken and
bruised them; the limes and lemons were good, but I could
bring only a few.

The next day being the 19th, I went back, having
made me two small bags to bring home my harvest; but
I was surprised, when, coming to my heap of grapes, I
found them all spread about and trod to pieces, an abundance eaten and devoured. By this I concluded there were
some wild creatures thereabouts which had done this. As
there was no laying them up in heaps, and no carrying
them away in a sack, I hung a large quantity of the grapes

upon the outer branches of the trees, that they might dry in the sun; as for the limes and lemons, I carried as many back as I could.

When I came home from this journey, I contemplated with great pleasure the fruitfulness of that valley and the pleasantness of the situation, the security from storms on that side, the water and the wood, and concluded that I had pitched upon a place to fix my abode in which was by far the worst part of the country. Upon the whole, I began to consider moving my habitation.

This thought ran long in my head, tempting me; but then I considered that I was now by the seaside, where it was at least possible that I might hail a ship driven from its course, though it was scarce probable that any such thing should ever happen. Yet to enclose myself among the hills and woods in the center of the island was to render such an affair impossible, and that therefore I ought not by any means to remove. However, I was so enamored of this place that I spent much of my time there for the whole remaining part of the month of July; and built me a little bower and surrounded it at a distance with a strong fence, being a double hedge, as high as I could reach, well staked and filled between with brushwood. Here I lay very secure sometimes two or three nights together, always going over the fence with a ladder, so that I fancied now I had my country and my seacoast house. This work took me up till the beginning of August.

I had but newly finished my fence and began to enjoy

my labor, when the rains came on and made me stick close to my first habitation; for though I had made a tent like the other, with a piece of sail, and spread it very well, yet I had not the shelter of a hill to keep me from storms, nor a cave behind me to retreat into.

By the 3rd of August the grapes I had hung up were perfectly dried and were excellent good raisins of the sun; so I began to take them down from the trees and was very happy that I did so, as the rains which followed would have spoiled them, and I should have lost the best part of my winter food, for I had above two hundred large bunches of them. No sooner had I taken them all down and carried most of them home to my cave, but it began to rain; and from hence, which was the 14th of August, it rained, more or less, every day till the middle of October; and sometimes so violently that I could not stir out of my cave for several days.

In this season, I was much surprised with the increase of my family. I had been concerned for the loss of one of my cats, who ran away from me or, as I thought, had been dead; till, to my astonishment, she came home about the end of August with three kittens. This was the more strange to me, both of my cats being females. I had, however, killed a wildcat, as I called it, with my gun, yet I had thought it was quite a different kind from our European cats.

From the 14th of August to the 26th, incessant rain, so that I could not stir, and was now very careful not to be much wet. In this confinement, I began to be straitened for food; but venturing out twice, I one day killed a goat, and the last day, which was the 24th, found a very large tortoise, which was a treat to me. My food was now regulated thus: I ate a bunch of raisins for my breakfast, a piece of the goat's flesh or of the turtle, broiled, for my dinner (for, to my great misfortune, I had no vessel to boil or stew anything), and two or three of the turtle's eggs for my supper.

SEPTEMBER 30. I was now come to the unhappy anniversary of my landing; I cast up the notches on my post and found I had been on shore three hundred and sixty-five days. I kept this day as a solemn fast, setting it apart for religious exercise, prostrating myself on the ground with the most serious humiliation, confessing my sins to God, acknowledging His righteous judgments upon me, and praying to Him to have mercy on me through Jesus Christ. And having not tasted the least refreshment for twelve hours, even till the going down of the sun, I then ate a biscuit and a bunch of grapes and went to bed. I had all this time observed no Sabbath day; for, as at first I had no sense of religion upon my mind, I had, after some time, omitted to distinguish the weeks by making a longer notch than ordinary for the Sabbath day, and so did not really know what any of the days were; but now, having cast up the days and found I had been there a year, I divided the year into weeks and set apart every seventh day for a Sabbath; though I found, at the end of my account, I had lost a day in my reckoning. A little after this, my ink beginning to fail me, I contented myself to write down only the most remarkable events of my life, without continuing a daily memorandum of other things.

The rainy season and the dry season began now to appear regular to me, and I learned to divide them so as to provide for them; but I bought all my experience before I had it, and what I am going to relate was one of the most discouraging experiments I had made.

I have mentioned that I had saved a few ears of the barley and rice, which I had so surprisingly found sprung up. There were about thirty stalks of rice and about twenty of barley, and now I thought it a proper time to sow it after the rains, the sun being in its southern position, going from me. Accordingly I dug a piece of ground, as well as I could, with my wooden spade, and dividing it into two parts, I sowed my grain; but as I was sowing, it occurred to my thoughts that I would not sow it all at first, because I did not know when was the proper time; so I sowed about two thirds of the seed, leaving about a handful of each, and it was a great comfort to me afterwards that I did so, for not one grain of what I sowed this time came to anything; for, the dry months following, the seed had no moisture to assist its growth.

I sowed the rest of my seed in February, a little before the vernal equinox. This, having the rainy months of March and April to water it, sprung up very pleasantly and yielded a good crop; but having only part of the seed left and not daring to sow all that I had, my whole crop did

2.5 gal / 2

not amount to above half a peck of each kind. But by this experiment I was made master of my business and knew exactly when to sow, and that I might expect two seed-times and two harvests every year.

About the month of November, I made a visit up the country to my bower, where, though I had not been for some months, yet I found all things just as I had left them. The circle or double hedge that I had made was not only firm and entire but the stakes, which I had cut out of some trees that grew thereabouts, were all shot out and grown with long branches. I was surprised and yet very well pleased to see the young trees grow, and I pruned them and led them to grow as much alike as I could; and it is scarce credible how beautiful a figure they grew into in three years, so that, though the hedge made a circle of about twenty-five yards in diameter, yet the trees, for such I might call them, soon covered it, and it was a complete shade, sufficient to lodge under all the dry season. This made me resolve to cut some more stakes and make me a hedge like this in a semicircle round the wall of my first dwelling, which I did; and placing the trees or stakes in a double row, at about eight yards distance from my first fence, they grew presently and were at first fine cover to my habitation.

❧❘ CHAPTER 9 ❘❧

I FOUND now that the year might be divided into rainy seasons and dry seasons, which were generally thus: from the middle of February to the middle of April, rainy, the sun being on or near the equinox; from the middle of April till the middle of August, dry, the sun being north of the Line; from the middle of August till the middle of October, rainy, the sun being come back to the Line; from the middle of October till the middle of February, dry, the sun being south of the Line.

After I had found, by experience, the ill consequences of being abroad in the rain, I sat within doors as much as possible during the wet months. During one of these times, I tried many ways to make myself a basket; but all the twigs I could get for the purpose proved so brittle that they would do nothing. It proved of excellent advantage to me now that when I was a boy, I used to take great delight in standing at a basketmaker's in the town where my father lived, to see them make their wickerware; and being, as boys usually are, a great observer of the manner how they worked those things, and sometimes lending a hand, I had full knowledge of the methods of it, so that I wanted nothing but the materials, when it came into my mind that the twigs of that tree from whence I cut my stakes that grew might possibly be as tough as the willows and osiers in England.

Accordingly, during the next dry season, I went with a hatchet to my country house, as I called it; and cutting some of the smaller twigs, I found them to my purpose as much as I could desire, whereupon I cut down a quantity. These I set up to dry within my hedge, and when they were fit for use, I carried them to my cave; and here I employed myself in making, as well as I could, several baskets, both to carry earth or to carry or lay up anything as I had occasion for. Though I did not finish them very handsomely, yet I made them sufficiently serviceable for my purpose; and thus, afterwards, I took care never to be without them; and especially strong deep baskets, to place my grain in, instead of sacks, when I should come to have any quantity of it. I employed myself in planting my second row of stakes or piles, and also in this wickerworking all the summer or dry season, when another business took me up more time than it could be imagined I could spare.

I mentioned before that I had a great mind to see the whole island, and that I had traveled up the brook, and so on to where I had built my bower, and where I had an opening to the sea, on the other side of the island. I now resolved to travel quite across to the seashore on that side; so, taking my gun, a hatchet, and my dog, and a larger quantity of powder and shot than usual, with two biscuit cakes and a great bunch of raisins in my pouch for my store, I began my journey. When I had passed the vale where my bower stood, I came within view of the sea to the west; and it being a clear day, I fairly descried land, whether an island or continent I could not tell; but it lay very high, extending from west to west-southwest about fifteen or twenty leagues off. I knew that this land must be part of America; and that if it was the Spanish coast, I should certainly, one time or other, see some vessel pass or repass one way or other; but if not, then it was the savage coast between the Spanish country and the Brazils, whose inhabitants are cannibals and fail not to murder and devour all human beings that fall into their hands.

Walking very leisurely forward, I found the open fields sweetly adorned with flowers and grass, and full of fine woods. I saw abundance of parrots and, after taking some pains, caught a young one and brought it home; but it was some years before I could make him speak.

I was exceedingly amused with this journey. I found in the low grounds hares and foxes, but they differed greatly from all the other kinds I had met with; nor could I satisfy myself to eat them, though I killed several. But I had no need to be venturous, for I had no want of food, and of that which was very good too, especially these three sorts, viz., goats, pigeons and turtle. With these, added to my grapes, Leadenhall market could not have furnished a table better than I, in proportion to the company; and though my case was deplorable enough, yet I was not driven to any extremities for food, but had rather plenty, even to dainties.

I never traveled above two miles outright in a day, or thereabout, but I took so many turns and returns to see what discoveries I could make that I came weary enough to the place where I resolved to sit down for the night; then I either reposed myself in a tree, or surrounded myself with a row of stakes, set upright in the ground, either from one tree to another, or so as no wild creature could come at me without waking me.

As soon as I came to the seashore, I saw that I had taken up my lot on the worst side of the island, for here the shore was covered with innumerable turtles, whereas, on the other side, I had found but three in a year and a half. Here was also an infinite number of fowls of many kinds, some of which I had not seen before and knew not the names of. I could have shot as many as I pleased but was very sparing of my powder and shot, and therefore had more mind to kill a she-goat, if I could, which I could better feed on. But, though there were more goats here than on my side the island, yet it was with much more difficulty that I could come near them, the country being flat and even, and they saw me much sooner than when I was upon a hill.

This side of the country was much pleasanter than mine, yet I had not the least inclination to remove; for as I was fixed in my habitation, it became natural to me, and I seemed all the while I was here to be upon a journey from home. However, I traveled along the seashore towards the east, I suppose about twelve miles; and then, setting up a great pole upon the shore for a mark, I concluded I would go home again; and that the next journey I took should be on the other side of the island, east from my dwelling, and so round till I came to my post again, of which in its place.

I took another way to come back than that I went; and in this journey, my dog surprised a young kid and seized upon it; and, running to take hold of it, I caught it and saved it alive from the dog. I had a great mind to bring it home, for I had often been musing whether it might not be possible to get a kid or two, and so raise a breed of tame goats, which might supply me when my powder and shot should be all spent. I made a collar for this little creature, and with a string which I had made of some rope yarn, which I always carried about me, I led him along, though with some difficulty, till I came to my bower, and there I enclosed and left him, for I was very impatient to be at home, from whence I had been absent above a month.

I cannot express what a satisfaction it was to me to come into my old hutch and lie down in my hammock bed. This little wandering journey, without a settled place of abode, made my own house, as I called it to myself, seem a perfect settlement; and it rendered everything about me so comfortable that I resolved I would never go a great way from it again while it should be my lot to stay on the island.

I reposed myself here a week, to rest and regale myself; during which most of the time was taken up in the weighty affair of making a cage for my Poll, who began now to be more domestic and to be mighty well acquainted with me. Then I began to think of the poor kid which I had penned within my little circle, and resolved to fetch it home. I found it almost starved for want of food. I cut boughs of trees, and branches of such shrubs as I could find, and threw it over, and having fed it, I tied it as before, to lead it away; but it was so tame with being hungry that I had no need to have tied it, for it followed me like a dog; and as I continually fed it, the creature became so loving, so gentle, and so fond that it would never leave me afterwards.

THE rainy season of the autumnal equinox was now come, and I kept the 30th of September in the same solemn manner as before, being the anniversary of my landing on the island; having now been there two years, and no more prospect of being delivered than the first day I came here. I spent the whole day in humble and thankful acknowledgments for the many wonderful mercies which my solitary condition was attended with, and without which it might have been infinitely more miserable. I gave humble and hearty thanks to God for having been pleased to discover to me that it was possible I might be more happy even in this solitary condition than I should have been in the enjoyment of society, and in all the pleasures of the world; that He could fully make up to me the deficiencies of my solitary state by His presence, and the communications of His grace to my soul; supporting, comforting, and encouraging me to depend upon His providence here, and to hope for His eternal presence hereafter.

It was now that I began sensibly to feel how much more happy the life I now led was, with all its miserable circumstances, than the wicked life I led all the past part of my days; and now I changed both my sorrows and my joys. Before, as I walked about, either on my hunting or for viewing the country, the anguish of my soul at my condition would break out upon me on a sudden, and make me wring my hands and weep like a child; sometimes it would take me in the middle of my work, and I would immediately sit down and sigh, and look upon the ground for an hour or two together.

But now, in a new disposition of mind, I began my third year; and, though I have not given the reader the trouble of so particular an account of my works this year as the first, yet in general it may be observed that I was seldom idle. But having regularly divided my time, according to the several daily employments that were before me; such as, first, my duty to God and the reading the Scriptures, which I constantly set apart some time for, thrice every day; secondly, going abroad with my gun or food, which generally took me up three hours every morning, when it did not rain; thirdly, ordering, curing, preserving, and cooking what I had killed or catched; these took up a great part of the day. Also it is to be considered that in the middle of the day, when the sun was in the zenith, the heat was too great to stir out.

I was now in the months of November and December, expecting my crop of barley and rice. My crop promised well, when, on a sudden, I found I was in danger of losing it all again by enemies of several sorts, which it was scarce possible to keep from it; as, first, the goats, and wild creatures which I called hares, who, tasting the sweetness of the blade, lay in it night and day, as soon as it came up, and ate it so close that it could get no time to shoot up into stalk.

I saw no remedy for this but by making an enclosure about it with a hedge, which I did with a great deal of toil. However, as my arable land was but small, I got it tolerably well fenced in about three weeks' time; and shooting some of the creatures in the daytime, I set my dog to guard it in the night, tying him up to a stake at the gate, where he would stand and bark all night long; so in a little time the enemies forsook the place, and the grain grew very strong and well, and began to ripen apace.

But now the birds were likely to ruin me; for, going along by the place to see how it throve, I saw my little crop surrounded with fowls, I know not of how many sorts, who stood, as it were, watching till I should be gone. I immediately let fly among them (for I always had my gun with me); I had no sooner shot but there rose up a little cloud of fowls, which I had not seen at all, from among the grain itself. This touched me sensibly, for I foresaw that in a few days they would devour all my hopes; that I should be starved and never be able to raise a crop at all; and I resolved I should watch my grain night and day. In the first place, I went among it to see what damage was already done and found they had spoiled a good deal of it; but that as it was yet too green for them, the loss was not so great but that the remainder was likely to be a good crop if it could be saved.

I stayed by it to load my gun, and then coming away, I could see the thieves sitting upon all the trees about me, as if they only waited till I was gone; and the event proved it to be so, for as I walked off, they dropped down, one by one, into the grain again. I was greatly provoked, knowing that every grain they ate now was, as it might be said, a peck loaf to me in the consequence; so, coming up to the hedge, I fired again and killed three of them. I took them up and served them as we serve notorious thieves in England, viz., hanged them in chains for a terror to others. It is impossible to imagine that this should have such an effect as it had; for the fowls not only never came to the grain, but they forsook all that part of the island, and I could never see a bird near the place as long as my scarecrows hung there. This I was very glad of, you may be sure;

and about the latter end of December, which was our second harvest of the year, I reaped my grain.

I was sadly put to it for a scythe to cut it down; and all I could do was to make one, as well as I could, out of one of the broadswords which I saved among the arms out of the ship. I cut nothing off but the ears, and carried it away in a great basket which I had made, and so rubbed it out with my hands; and at the end of all my harvesting, I found that out of my half peck of seed I had near two bushels of rice, and above two bushels and a half of barley. This was great encouragement to me; and I foresaw that, in time, it would please God to supply me with bread; and yet here I was perplexed again, for I neither knew how to grind or make meal of my grain or, indeed, how to clean it and part it; nor, if made into meal, how to make bread of it. I resolved not to taste any of this crop, but to preserve it all for seed against the next season; and, in the meantime, to employ all my study and hours of working to provide myself with grain and bread.

It is a little wonderful, and what I believe few people have thought much upon, viz., the strange multitude of little things necessary in the providing this one article of bread. I, who was reduced to a mere state of nature, was made more sensible of this every hour. First, I had no plow to turn up the earth, and only a spade to dig it. When the grain was sown, I had no harrow, but was forced to drag a great heavy bough of a tree over it, to scratch it, as it may be called, rather than harrow it. When it was growing and grown, I wanted many things to fence it, secure it, mow or reap it, cure and carry it home, thresh it and save it; then I was without a mill to grind it, sieves to dress it, yeast to make it into bread, and an oven to bake it. I had the next six months to apply myself wholly, by labor and invention, to furnish myself with utensils proper for the performing all these operations.

✥ CHAPTER 10 ✥

NOW I was to prepare more land, for I had seed enough to sow above an acre of ground. Before I did this, I had a week's work at least to make me a new spade; which, when it was done, was but a sorry one indeed, and very heavy, and required double labor to work with it. However, I went through that, and sowed my seed in two large flat pieces of ground, as near my house as I could find them, and fenced them in with a good hedge, the stakes of which were all cut off that wood which I had set before, and knew it would grow into a living hedge that would want but little repair. This work took me up full three months, because a great part of the time was in the wet season, when I could not go abroad.

When it rained and I could not go out, I diverted myself while at work with talking to my parrot and teaching him to speak; and I quickly taught him to know his own name, and at last to speak it out pretty loud, "Poll"; which was the first word I ever heard spoken in the island by any mouth but my own. This was not my work, but an assistant to my work: for now I had a great employment upon my hands. I had long studied to make myself some earthen vessels, for I had no vessel to hold anything that was liquid, except two runlets which were almost full of rum, and some glass bottles, some of the common size, and others (which were case bottles) square, for the holding of waters, spirits, etc. I had not so much as a pot to boil anything, except a great kettle which I saved out of the ship, and which was too big for such use as I desired it, viz., to make broth and stew a bit of meat.

Considering the heat of the climate, I did not doubt but if I could find out any clay, I might botch up some such pot as might, being dried in the sun, be hard and strong enough to bear handling, and to hold anything that was dry, and required to be kept so; and as this was necessary in the preparing flour, meal, etc., I resolved to make some as large as I could, and fit only to stand like jars, to hold what should be put into them.

It would make the reader pity me, or rather laugh at me, to tell how many awkward ways I took to raise this paste; what odd, misshapen, ugly things I made; how many of them fell in and how many fell out, the clay not being stiff enough to bear its own weight; how many cracked by the over-violent heat of the sun, being set out too hastily; and how many fell in pieces before or after they were dried;

and how, after having labored hard to find the clay, to dig it, to temper it, to bring it home and work it, I could not make above two large earthen ugly things (I cannot call them jars) in about two months' labor.

However, as the sun baked these two very dry and hard, I lifted them gently up and set them down again in two great wicker baskets, which I had made on purpose for them that they might not break; and as between the pot and the basket there was a little room to spare, I stuffed it full of the rice and barley straw; and these two pots being to stand always dry, I thought would hold my dry grain and perhaps the meal.

I made several smaller things with better success; such as little round pots, flat dishes, pitchers, and small jars, or pipkins; and the heat of the sun baked them strangely hard.

But all this would not answer my end, which was to get an earthen pot to hold liquids and bear the fire, which none of these could do. It happened some time after, making a pretty large fire for cooking my meat, when I went to put it out after I had done with it, I found a broken piece of one of my earthenware vessels in the fire, burned as hard as a stone and red as a tile. I was agreeably surprised to see it, and set myself to study how they might be made to burn whole since they would burn broken.

I placed three pipkins and two or three pots in a pile, one upon another, and placed my firewood all round it, with a great heap of embers under them. I plied the fire with fresh fuel round the outside and upon the top till I saw the pots in the inside red-hot quite through and observed that they did not crack at all; when I saw them clear red, I let them stand in that heat about five or six hours, till I found one of them, though it did not crack, did melt or run; for the sand which was mixed with the clay melted by the violence of the heat and would have run into glass if I had gone on; so I slacked my fire gradually till the pots began to abate of the red color, and watched them all night that I might not let the fire abate too fast. In the morning I had three very good, I will not say handsome, pipkins, and two earthen pots, as hard burned as could be desired; and one of them perfectly glazed with the running of the sand.

After this experiment, I wanted no sort of earthenware for my use; but, as to the shapes of them, they were very indifferent. No joy at a thing of so mean a nature was ever equal to mine, when I found I had made an earthen pot that would bear the fire; and I had hardly patience to stay till they were cold, before I set one on the fire again, with some water in it, to boil me some meat, which it did admirably well; and with a piece of a kid I made some very good broth.

My next concern was to get a stone mortar to stamp or beat some grain in. I spent many a day to find out a stone big enough to cut hollow and make fit for a mortar; but could find none at all, except what was in the solid rock and which I had no way to cut out; nor, indeed, were the rocks in the island of sufficient hardness, as they were all of a sandy, crumbling stone. So, after a great deal of time lost in searching for a stone, I gave it over and resolved to seek out a block of hard wood, which I found indeed much easier; and, getting one as big as I had strength to stir, I rounded it and formed it on the outside with my axe and hatchet; and then, with the help of the fire and infinite labor, made a hollow place in it, as the Indians in Brazil make their canoes. After this, I made a great heavy pestle of the wood called ironwood.

My next difficulty was to make a sieve to part my meal from the bran and the husk. This was a most difficult thing, even to think on, for I had nothing like the necessary thing to make it; I mean fine thin canvas or stuff to search the meal through. Linen I had none left but what was mere rags; I had goats' hair, but neither knew how to weave it nor spin it; and, had I known how, here were no tools to work it with. At last, recollecting I had, among the seamen's clothes which were saved out of the ship, some neckcloths of calico or muslin, with some pieces of these I made three small sieves, proper enough for the work.

The baking part was the next thing to be considered; for, first, I had no yeast. As there was no supplying that want, I did not concern myself much about it; but for an oven I was indeed puzzled. At length I found out an expedient, which was this: I made some earthen vessels, about two feet diameter and not above nine inches deep; these I burned in the fire and laid them by; and when I wanted to bake, I made a great fire upon my hearth, which I had paved with some square tiles of my own making; but I should not call them square. When the firewood was burned into embers, I let them lie till the hearth was very hot; then, sweeping them away, I set down my loaves and, covering them with the earthen pot, drew the embers all around the outside of the pot to keep in the heat; and thus, as well as in the best oven in the world, I baked my barley loaves and made several cakes and puddings of the rice.

It need not be wondered at if all these things took me up most part of the third year of my abode here; for, in the intervals of these things, I had my new harvest and husbandry to manage; I reaped my grain in its season, and carried it home, and laid it up in my large baskets. The increase of the grain now yielded me so much that I had of the barley and of rice about twenty bushels each, so that now I resolved to use it freely. I resolved also to sow the same quantity every year that I sowed the last, on hopes that such a quantity would fully provide me with bread, etc.

ALL the while these things were doing, you may be sure my thoughts ran many times upon the prospect of land which I had seen from the other side of the island; and I was not without some secret wishes that I was on shore there, fancying that I might find some way or other to convey myself farther and perhaps at last find some means of escape.

But all this while I made no allowance for the dangers of

such a condition, and that I should run a hazard of more than a thousand to one of being killed and eaten; for the people of the Caribbean coast were cannibals; and I knew, by the latitude that I could not be far off from that shore. Then supposing they were not cannibals, yet that they might kill me, as they had many Europeans who had fallen into their hands, even when they have been ten or twenty together; and I was but one, and could make little or no defense; all these things I ought to have considered well of, yet my head ran mightily upon the thought of getting over to the shore.

After several weeks, I began to think whether it was not possible to make myself a canoe, or periagua, such as the natives of those climates make with the trunk of a great tree. I went to work upon this boat the most like a fool that ever man did who had any of his senses awake. I felled a cedar tree, and I question much whether Solomon ever had such a one for the building of the Temple at Jerusalem; it was five feet ten inches diameter at the lower part next the stump, and four feet eleven inches diameter at the end of twenty-two feet, where it lessened and parted into branches. It was not without infinite labor that I felled this tree; I was twenty days hacking and hewing at the bottom, and fourteen more getting the branches and limbs cut off. After this, it cost me a month to shape it to something like the bottom of a boat, that it might swim upright. It cost me near three months more to clear the inside and work it out so as to make an exact boat of it; this I did, indeed, without fire, by mere mallet and chisel, and by the dint of hard labor, till I had brought it to be a very handsome periagua, and big enough to have carried six and twenty men, really much bigger than ever I saw a canoe that was made of one tree.

But all my devices to get it into the water failed me, though they cost me inexpressible labor too. It lay about one hundred yards from the water, not more; but it was uphill towards the creek. Well, I resolved to dig into the surface of the earth, and so make a declivity; this I began, and it cost me a prodigious deal of pains (but who grudge pains that have their deliverance in view?). When this was done, I still could not stir the canoe. Then I resolved to cut a canal to bring the water up to the canoe, seeing I could not bring the canoe down to the water. But when I calculated how deep it was to be dug, how broad, how the stuff was to be thrown out, I found by the number of hands I had, having none but my own, that it must have been ten or twelve years before I could have gone through with it. So, at length, though with great reluctancy, I was obliged to give over.

This grieved me heartily; and now I saw, though too late, the folly of beginning a work before we count the cost, and before we judge rightly of our own strength to go through with it.

In the middle of this work I finished my fourth year in this place, and kept my anniversary with the same devotion, and with as much comfort as before; for, by a constant study and serious application to the word of God and by the assistance of His grace, I gained a different knowledge from what I had before; I entertained different notions of things; I looked now upon the world as a thing remote, which I had nothing to do with, no expectation from, and, indeed, no desires about.

I was here removed from all the wickedness of the world; I had neither the lust of the flesh, the lust of the eye, nor the pride of life. I had nothing to covet, for I had all that I was now capable of enjoying: I was lord of the whole manor; or, if I pleased, I might call myself king or emperor over the whole country which I had possession of; there were no rivals; I had no competitor, none to dispute sovereignty with me. I might have raised ship-loadings of grain, but I had no use for it; so I let as little grow as I thought enough for my occasion. I had turtles enough, but now and then one was as much as I could put to any use; I had timber enough to have built a fleet of ships, and I had grapes enough to have made wine, or to have cured into raisins, to have loaded that fleet when it had been built.

In a word, just reflection dictated to me that all the good things of this world are of no farther good to us than for our use; and that whatever we may heap up, we enjoy only as much as we can use and no more. The most covetous miser in the world would have been cured of covetousness if he had been in my case, for I possessed infinitely more than I knew what to do with. I had, as I hinted before, a parcel of money, as well gold as silver, about thirty-six pounds sterling. Alas! There the sorry, useless stuff lay; I had no manner of business for it; and I often thought within myself that I would have given a handful of it for a gross of tobacco pipes or for a hand mill to grind my corn; nay, I would have given it all for a sixpennyworth of turnip and carrot seed from England or for a handful of peas and beans and a bottle of ink. As it was, I had not the least advantage by it, or benefit from it; but there it lay in a drawer and grew moldy with the damp of the cave in the wet seasons; and if I had had the drawer full of diamonds, it had been the same case; they would have been of no manner of value to me because of no use.

I had now brought my state of life to be much more comfortable in itself than it was at first, and much easier to my mind, as well as to my body. I frequently sat down to meat with thankfulness and admired the hand of God's providence, which had thus spread my table in the wilderness; I learned to look more upon the bright side of my condition, and less upon the dark side, and to consider what I enjoyed rather than what I wanted; and this gave me sometimes such secret comforts that I cannot express them; and which I take notice of here, to put those discontented people in mind of it, who cannot enjoy comfortably what God has given them, because they see and covet something that He has not given them. All our discontents appeared to me to spring from the want of thankfulness for what we have.

Another reflection was of great use to me, and doubt-less would be so to anyone that should fall into such distress as mine; and this was to compare my present con-dition with what I at first expected it would be; nay, with what it would have been if the good providence of God had not wonderfully ordered the ship to be cast up where I not only could come at her but could bring what I got out of her to the shore for my relief and comfort.

I spent whole hours, I may say whole days, in represent-ing to myself, in the most lively colors, how I must have acted if I had got nothing out of the ship. I could not have got any food, except fish and turtles; I should have lived, if I had not perished, like a mere savage; if I had killed a goat or a fowl by any contrivance, I had no way to open it, or part the flesh from the skin, or to cut it up, but must gnaw it with my teeth and pull it with my claws like a beast.

These reflections made me very sensible of the goodness of Providence to me, and very thankful for my present condition, with all its hardships and misfortunes; and this part also I cannot but recommend to the reflection of those who are apt, in their misery, to say, Is any affliction like mine? Let them consider how much worse the cases of some people are, and their case might have been, if Provi-dence had thought fit.

I HAD now been here so long that many things which I brought on shore for my help were either quite gone, or very much wasted.

My ink had been gone for some time, all but a very little, which I eked out with water, a little and a little, till it was so pale it scarce left any appearance of black upon the paper. As long as it lasted, I made use of it to minute down the days of the month on which any remarkable thing happened to me.

My clothes, too, began to decay mightily: as to linen, I had none for a great while, except some checkered shirts which I found in the chests of the other seamen, and which I carefully preserved, because many times I could bear no clothes on but a shirt, and it was a very great help to me that I had, among all the men's clothes of the ship, almost three dozen of shirts. There were also several thick watch coats of the seamen's, but they were too hot to wear; and, though it is true that the weather was so violently hot that there was no need of clothes, yet I could not go quite naked. The reason why I could not was that the very heat frequently blistered my skin; whereas, with a shirt on, the air itself made some motion, and whistling under the shirt was twofold cooler than without it. No more could I go out in the heat of the sun without a cap or hat on; the heat of the sun beating with such violence, as it does in that place, would give me the headache presently, by darting so directly upon my head that I could not bear it.

Upon these views, I began to consider about putting the few rags I had, which I called clothes, into some order. I had worn out all the waistcoats I had, and my business was now to try if I could not make jackets out of the great watch coats; so I set to work a-tailoring, or rather, indeed, a-botching, for I made most piteous work of it. However, I made three new waistcoats, which I hoped would serve me a great while; as for breeches, or drawers, I made but a very sorry shift indeed, till afterwards.

I had saved the skins of all the creatures that I killed, I mean four-footed ones; and I had hung them up, stretched out with sticks in the sun, by which means some of them were so dry and hard that they were fit for little, but others I found very useful. The first thing I made of these was a great cap for my head, with the hair on the outside, to shoot off the rain; and this I performed so well that after this I made me a suit of clothes wholly of the skins, that is to say, a waistcoat and breeches, open at the knees and both loose; for they were rather wanting to keep me cool than warm. I must not omit to acknowledge that they were wretchedly made; for if I was a bad carpenter, I was a worse tailor. However, they were such as I made very good shift with; and when I was abroad, if it happened to rain, the hair of my waistcoat and cap being uppermost, I was kept very dry.

After this, I spent a great deal of time and pains to make an umbrella; I was indeed in great want of one, and I had seen them made in the Brazils, where they were very useful in the great heats, and I felt the heats every jot as great here; besides, as I was obliged to be much abroad, it was a most useful thing to me, as well for the rains as the heats. I took a world of pains at it, and at last I made one that answered indifferently well. The main difficulty was to make it to let down; I could make it spread, but if it did not let down too, and draw in, it was not portable for me any way but just over my head. However, at last, I made one to answer and covered it with skins, the hair upwards, so that it cast off the rain and kept off the sun so effectually that I could walk out in the hottest of the weather with greater advantage than I could before in the coolest; and when I had no need of it, could close it and carry it under my arm.

Thus I lived mighty comfortably, my mind being entirely composed by God's providence. When I began to regret the want of conversation, I would ask myself whether thus conversing mutually with my own thoughts and, as I hope I may say, with even God Himself, by exclamations, was not better than the utmost enjoyment of human society!

⊰❧ CHAPTER 11 ❦⊱

AFTER this, or five years, I lived on in the same course as before; besides my yearly labor of planting my barley and rice and curing my raisins, and my daily going out with my gun, I had one labor, to make me a smaller canoe, which at last I finished. By digging a canal to it of six feet wide and four feet deep, I brought it into the creek, almost half a mile.

My next design was to make a cruise round the island. I fitted up a little mast in my boat and made a sail to it out of some of the pieces of the ship's sails. Then I made lockers, or boxes, at each end of my boat, to put provisions, ammunition, etc., into to be kept dry, either from rain or the spray of the sea; and a long hollow place I cut in the inside of the boat, where I could lay my gun, making a flap to hang down over it. I fixed my umbrella also in a step at the stern, like a mast, to stand over my head and keep the heat of the sun off me, like an awning; and I victualed my ship, putting in two dozen loaves of barley bread, an earthen pot full of parched rice, a little bottle of rum, half a goat, and powder and shot for killing more, and two large watch coats, one to lie upon and the other to cover me in the night.

It was the sixth of November, in the sixth year of my reign, or my captivity, which you please, that I set out on this voyage, and I found it much longer than I expected; for, though the island itself was not very large, yet when I came to the east side of it, I found a great ledge of rocks lie out about two leagues into the sea, so that I was obliged to go a great way out to sea to double the point.

No sooner was I come to the point, when I was not even my boat's length from the shore, but I found myself in a great depth of water, and a current like the sluice of a mill; it carried my boat along with such violence that all I could do could not keep her so much as on the edge of it; but I found it hurried me farther and farther out from the eddy, which was on my left hand. There was no wind stirring to help me, and all I could do with my paddles signified nothing; and now I began to give myself over for lost, for I was being driven into the vast ocean.

And now I saw how easy it was for the providence of God to make even the most miserable condition of mankind worse. Now I looked back upon my desolate, solitary island as the most pleasant place in the world; and all the happiness my heart could wish for was to be but there again. I stretched out my hands to it with eager wishes: "Oh happy desert!" said I. "I shall never see thee more." It is scarce possible to imagine the consternation I was now in, being driven from my beloved island into the wide ocean. However, I worked hard, till indeed my strength was almost exhausted, and kept my boat as much to the northward, that is, towards the side of the current which the eddy lay on, as possible; when about noon, as the sun passed the meridian, I thought I felt a little breeze in my face, springing up from the south-southeast. This cheered my heart, and especially when, in about half an hour more, it blew a pretty gentle gale. By this time I was got at a frightful distance from the island, and had the least cloudy or hazy weather intervened, I had been undone another way too, for I had no compass on board and should never have known how to have steered towards the island if I had once lost sight of it; but the weather continuing clear, I applied myself to get up my mast again and spread my sail, standing away to the north as much as possible, to get out of the current.

Just as I had set my mast and sail, and the boat began to stretch away, I saw even by the clearness of the water some alteration of the current was near; for where the current was so strong, the water was foul. And presently I found to the east, at about half a mile, a breach of the sea upon some rocks; these rocks I found caused the current to part again, and as the main stress of it ran away more southerly, leaving the rocks to the northeast, so the other returned by the repulse of the rocks and made a strong eddy again to the northwest with a very sharp stream.

They who know what it is to be rescued from thieves just going to murder them, or who have been in suchlike extremities, may guess with what joy I put my boat into the stream of this eddy; and the wind, also freshening, how gladly I spread my sail to it, running cheerfully before the wind, and with a strong tide or eddy underfoot.

About four o'clock in the evening, being then within a league of the island, I found the point of rocks which occasioned this disaster. Having still a wind fair for me, I got around it and, in about an hour, came within about a mile of the shore, where, it being smooth water, I soon got to land.

When I was on shore, I fell on my knees and gave God thanks for my deliverance; and refreshing myself with such things as I had, I brought my boat close to the shore, in a little cove that I had spied under some trees, and laid me down to sleep, being quite spent with the labor and fatigue of the voyage.

I was now at a great loss which way to get home with my boat; I had run too much hazard to think of attempting it by the way I went out, so I resolved in the morning to make my way westward along the shore and see if there was no creek where I might lay up my frigate in safety, so as to have her again if I wanted her. Coasting the shore, I came to a very good inlet, which narrowed till it came to a little brook, where I found a very convenient harbor for my boat, and where she lay as if she had been in a little dock made on purpose for her. Here I put in, and, having stowed my boat very safe, I went on shore to look about me.

I soon found I had but a little passed by the place where I had been before, when I traveled on foot to that shore; so taking nothing out of my boat but my gun and umbrella, for it was exceeding hot, I began my march. The way was comfortable enough after such a voyage as I had been upon, and I reached my old bower in the evening, where I found everything standing as I had left it. I got over the fence and laid me down in the shade to rest my limbs, for I was very weary, and fell asleep; but judge you, if you can that read my story, what a surprise I must be in when I was awaked out of my sleep by a voice, calling me by my name several times, "Robin, Robin, Robin Crusoe; poor Robin Crusoe! Where are you, Robin Crusoe? Where have you been?"

I started up in the utmost consternation, dreadfully frightened; but no sooner were my eyes open, but I saw my parrot sitting on the top of the hedge and immediately knew it was he that spoke to me; for just in such bemoaning language I had used to talk to him and teach him, and he had learned it perfectly.

However, even though I knew it was the parrot, and that indeed it could be nobody else, it was a good while before I could compose myself; and I was amazed how the creature got thither; but, at last, holding out my hand and calling him by his name, Poll, the sociable creature came to me, and sat upon my thumb, and continued talking to me, "Poor Robin Crusoe!" just as if he had been overjoyed to see me again; and so I carried him home.

I now had enough of rambling to sea for some time, and had enough to do for many days to sit still and to reflect upon the danger I had been in. I would have been very glad to have had my boat again on my side of the island; but I knew not how it was practicable to get it about. As to the east side of the island, which I had gone round, I knew well enough there was no venturing that way; my very heart would shrink, and my very blood run chill, but to think of it; and as to the other side of the island, I did not know how it might be there; but supposing the current ran with the same force against the shore at the east as it passed by it on the other, I might run the same risk of being carried by the island, as I had been before of being carried away from it; so with these thoughts, I contented myself to be without any boat, though it had been the product of so many months' labor to make it.

In this government of my temper I remained near a year, lived a very sedate, retired life, as you may well suppose, and very happily in all things, except that of society. I improved myself in this time in all the mechanic exercises which my necessities put me upon applying myself to; and I believe I could, upon occasion, have made a very good carpenter, especially considering how few tools I had.

But I think I was never more vain of my own perform-ance, or more joyful for anything I found out, than for my being able to make a tobacco pipe; and though it was a very ugly clumsy thing and only burned red, like other earthenware, yet as it was hard and firm and would draw the smoke, I was exceedingly comforted with it, for I had been always used to smoke.

I began now to perceive my powder abated considerably; this was a want which it was impossible for me to supply, and I began seriously to consider what I must do when I should have no more powder, that is to say, how I should do to kill any goats. I had, as is observed, in the third year of my being here, kept a young kid and bred her up tame, and I was in hopes of getting a he-goat; but I could not by any means bring it to pass till my kid grew an old goat; and as I could never find in my heart to kill her, she died at last of mere age.

BEING now in the eleventh year of my residence and, as I have said, my ammunition growing low, I set myself to study some art to trap and snare the goats, to see whether I could not catch some of them alive; and particularly, I wanted a she-goat great with young. For this purpose, I resolved to try a pitfall; so I dug several large pits in the earth, in places where I had observed the goats used to feed, and over those pits I placed hurdles, of my own making too, with a great weight upon them, and ears of barley and dry rice; and going one morning to see my traps, I found in one of them a large old he-goat, and in one of the others three kids.

As to the old one, I knew not what to do with him; he was so fierce I durst not go into the pit to bring him away alive, which was what I wanted. I could have killed him, but that was not my business, nor would it answer my end; so I let him out, and he ran away, as if he had been frightened out of his wits. But I had forgot then that hunger will tame a lion. If I had let him stay there three or four days without food, and then have carried him some water to drink, and then a little corn, he would have been as tame as one of the kids; for they are mighty sagacious, tractable creatures, where they are well used. However, I let him go; then I went to the three kids, and taking them one by one, I tied them with strings together, and with some difficulty brought them all home.

It was a good while before they would feed; but throwing them some sweet corn, it tempted them, and they began to be tame. And now I found that if I expected to supply myself with goat's flesh when I had no powder or shot left, breeding some up tame was my only way, when, perhaps, I might have them about my house like a flock of sheep. But then it occurred to me that I must keep the tame from the wild, or else they would run wild when they grew up; and the only way for this was to have some enclosed piece of ground, well hedged, so that those within might not break out or those without break in.

This was a great undertaking for one pair of hands; yet as I saw there was an absolute necessity for doing it, my first work was to find out a proper piece of ground, where there was likely to be herbage for them to eat, water for them to drink, and cover to keep them from the sun. I pitched upon a place very proper for all these, being plain open meadowland, with two or three little drills of fresh water in it and at one end very woody.

For a beginning, I enclosed a piece of about one hundred and fifty yards in length and one hundred yards in breadth; to which, as my stock increased, I could add more ground.

This answered my end; and in about a year and a half I had a flock of about twelve goats, kids and all; and in two years more, I had three and forty, beside several that I took and killed for my food. After that I enclosed five other pieces of ground to feed them in, with little pens to drive them into, to take them as I wanted, and gates out of one piece of ground into another.

But this was not all; for now I not only had goat's flesh to feed on when I pleased, but milk too, sometimes a gallon or two in a day. And as Nature, who gives supplies of food to every creature, dictates naturally how to make use of it, so I, that had never milked a cow, much less a goat, or seen butter or cheese made, only when I was a boy, after a great many essays and miscarriages made me both butter and cheese at last and never wanted for them afterwards. How mercifully can our Creator treat His creatures, even in those conditions in which they seemed to be overwhelmed in destruction! What a table was here spread for me in a wilderness!

It would have made a stoic smile to have seen me and

my little family sit down to dinner. There was my majesty, the prince and lord of the whole island. I had the lives of all my subjects at my absolute command; I could hang, draw, give liberty, and take it away, and no rebels among all my subjects. Then to see how like a king I dined too, all alone, attended by my servants; Poll, as if he had been my favorite, was the only person permitted to talk to me. My dog, who was now grown very old and had found no species to multiply his kind upon, sat always at my right hand; and two cats, one on one side of the table and one on the other, expecting now and then a bit from my hand as a mark of special favor.

But these were not the two cats which I brought on shore at first, for they were both of them dead and had been interred near my habitation by my own hand; but one of them having multiplied by I know not what kind of creature, these were two which I had preserved tame, whereas the rest ran wild in the woods.

I WAS something impatient, as I have observed, to have the use of my boat, though very loath to run any more hazards; and I had a strange uneasiness in my mind to go back to the other side of the island. This inclination increased upon me every day, and at length I resolved to travel thither by land; following the edge of the shore, I did so. But had anyone in England been to meet such a man as I was, it must either have frightened him or raised a great deal of laughter; and as I frequently stood still to look at myself, I could not but smile at the notion of my traveling through Yorkshire with such an equipage and in such a dress. Be pleased to take a sketch of my figure, as follows:

I had a great high shapeless cap, made of a goat's skin, with a flap hanging down behind, as well to keep the sun from me as to shoot the rain off from running into my neck. I had a short jacket of goat's skin, the skirts coming down to about the middle of the thighs, and a pair of open-kneed breeches of the same; the breeches were made of the skin of an old he-goat, whose hair hung down such a length on either side that, like pantaloons, it reached to the middle of my legs; stockings and shoes I had none, but had made me a pair of somethings, I scarce know what to call them, like buskins, to flap over my legs, and lace on either side, but of a most barbarous shape, as indeed were all the rest of my clothes.

I had on a broad belt of goat's skin dried, which I drew together with two thongs of the same; and in a kind of a frog on either side of this, instead of a sword and dagger, hung a little saw and a hatchet; one on one side, and one on the other. I had another belt, not so broad, and fastened in the same manner, which hung over my shoulder; and at the end of it, under my left arm, hung two goat's-skin pouches, in one of which hung my powder, in the other my shot. At my back I carried my basket, on my shoulder my gun, and over my head a great clumsy ugly goat's-skin umbrella. As for my face, the color of it was really not so mulatto-like as one might expect from a man not at all careful of it and living within nine or ten degrees of the equator. My beard I had once suffered to grow till it was about a quarter of a yard long; but as I had both scissors and razors sufficient, I had cut it pretty short, except what grew on my upper lip, which I had trimmed into a large pair of Mahometan whiskers, such as I had seen worn by some Turks at Sallee. I will not say they were long enough to hang my hat upon, but they were of a monstrous length and shape, such as, in England, would have passed for frightful.

In this kind of figure I went my new journey, and was out five or six days. I traveled along the seashore, directly to the point of the rocks from which I had been carried out to sea by the current. I was surprised to see the sea all smooth and quiet, with no more current than in any other places. I was at a strange loss to understand this, but was presently convinced that the tide of ebb, joining with the waters from some great river, must be the occasion of this current at certain times of day.

This observation convinced me that I had nothing to do but to observe the ebbing and the flowing of the tide, and I might very easily bring my boat about the island again; but when I began to think of putting it in practice, I had such a terror upon my spirits at the remembrance of the danger I had been in that I took up another resolution, which was more safe, though more laborious; and this was that I would make me another canoe, and so have one for one side of the island and one for the other.

I now had, as I may call it, two plantations in the island:

one, my fortification or tent with the wall about it, with the cave behind me, which, by this time, I had enlarged into several apartments or caves, one within another, where I stored my provisions. Near this dwelling lay my two pieces of grainland, which I kept cultivated and sowed, and which duly yielded me their harvest in its season.

Besides this, I had my countryseat, and I had now a tolerable plantation there also; for, first, I had my little bower, which I kept in repair; that is to say, I kept the hedge which encircled it in constantly fitted up to its usual height, the ladder standing always in the inside; I kept the trees, which were now grown very firm and tall, always cut so that they might spread and grow thick, and make the more agreeable shade. In the middle of this I had my tent always standing, and under this I had made me a couch with the skins of the creatures I had killed.

Adjoining to my country habitation I had my enclosures for my goats, and in this place also I had my grapes growing. As this was about halfway between my other habitation and the place where I had laid up my boat, I generally lay here in my way thither; for I used frequently to visit my boat, and I kept her in very good order. Sometimes I went out in her to divert myself, but never above a stone's cast from the shore, I was so apprehensive of being hurried out of my knowledge again by the currents or winds— But now I come to a new scene of my life.

❧ CHAPTER 12 ❧

IT HAPPENED one day, about noon. Going towards my boat, I was exceedingly surprised with the print of a man's naked foot on the shore, which was very plain to be seen in the sand. I stood like one thunderstruck, or as if I had seen an apparition. I listened, I looked round me, but I could hear nothing, nor see anything; I went up to a rising ground to look farther; I went up the shore and down the shore, but I could see no other impression but that one. I went to it again to see if there were any more, and to observe if it might not be my fancy; but there was exactly the print of a foot, toes, heel, and every part of a foot. How it came thither I could not in the least imagine; but after innumerable fluttering thoughts, like a man perfectly confused, I came home to my fortification, not feeling the ground I went on but terrified to the last degree; looking behind me at every two or three steps, mistaking every bush and tree, and fancying every stump at a distance to be a man.

When I came to my castle (for so I called it ever after this), I fled into it like one pursued; whether I went over by the ladder or went in at the hole in the rock, which I had called a door, I cannot remember; for never frightened hare fled to cover, or fox to earth, with more terror of mind than I to this retreat.

I slept none that night; the farther I was from the occasion of my fright, the greater my apprehensions were, which is something contrary to the usual practice of all creatures in fear; but I was so embarrassed with my own frightful ideas of the thing that I formed nothing but dismal imaginations to myself. Sometimes I fancied it must be the Devil; for how should any other thing in human shape come into the place? Where was the vessel that brought them? What marks were there of any other footsteps? And how was it possible a man should come there? But then, to think that Satan should take human shape upon him in such a place, where there could be no occasion for it but to leave the print of his foot behind him; and that for no purpose too, for, as I lived on the other side of the island, it was ten thousand to one whether I should ever see it, and in the sand, which the first surge of the sea would have defaced; all this seemed inconsistent with the notions we usually entertain of the subtlety of the Devil.

So I presently concluded, then, that it must be some of the savages of the mainland over against me who had wandered out to sea in their canoes and, driven by the currents or by contrary winds, had made the island and had been on shore but were gone away again to sea; being as loath, perhaps, to have stayed in this desolate island as I would have been to have had them.

While these reflections were rolling upon my mind, I was very thankful in my thoughts that I had not been thereabouts at that time, or that they did not see my boat, by which they would have concluded that some inhabitants had been in the place, and perhaps have searched farther for me. If so, they would certainly come again in great numbers and devour me; that if it should happen that they should not find me, yet they would find my enclosure, destroy all my grain, and carry away my flock of tame goats, and I should perish at last for mere want.

Thus my fear banished all my religious hope, all that former confidence in God, which was founded upon such wonderful experience as I had had of His goodness, as if He that had fed me by miracle hitherto could not preserve, by His power, the provision which He had made for me by His goodness.

How strange a checkerwork of Providence is the life of man! Today we love what tomorrow we hate; today we seek what tomorrow we shun; today we desire what tomorrow we fear. This was exemplified in me at this time in the most lively manner; for I, whose only affliction was that I seemed banished from human society, that I was alone, circumscribed by the boundless ocean, cut off from mankind, and condemned to what I called silent life; that to have seen one of my own species would have seemed to me the greatest blessing that Heaven itself, next to the supreme blessing of salvation, could bestow; I say, that I should now tremble at the very apprehensions of seeing a man, and was ready to sink into the ground at but the shadow or silent appearance of a man's having set his foot in the island.

Such is the uneven state of human life; and it afforded me a great many curious speculations afterwards, when I had a little recovered my first surprise. I considered that this was the station of life the infinitely wise and good providence of God had determined for me; that as I could not foresee what the ends of divine wisdom might be in all this, so I was not to dispute His sovereignty; and it was my duty to hope in Him, pray to Him, and quietly to attend the dictates and directions of His daily providence.

These thoughts took me up many hours and days, and one particular effect of my cogitations I cannot omit. One morning, filled with thoughts about my danger from the appearance of savages, I took up my Bible, and opening it to read, the first words that presented to me were, *Wait on the Lord, and be of good courage, and He shall strengthen thine heart; wait, I say, on the Lord.* It is impossible to express the comfort this gave me. In answer, I thankfully laid down the book and was no more sad, at least on that occasion.

In the middle of these reflections, it came into my thoughts one day that all this might be a mere chimera of my own, and that this foot might be the print of my own foot, when I came on shore from my boat. This cheered me up a little too, and I began to persuade myself it was all a delusion.

Now I began to take courage and to peep abroad again, for I had not stirred out of my castle for three days and nights, so that I began to starve for provisions; for I had little or nothing withindoors but some barley cakes and water. Then I knew that my goats wanted to be milked, too, which usually was my evening diversion, and the poor creatures would be in great pain and inconvenience for want of it. Encouraging myself, therefore, with the belief that this was nothing but the print of one of my own feet, and that I might be truly said to start at my own shadow, I began to go abroad again, and went to my country house to milk my flock; but to see with what fear I went forward, how often I looked behind me, how I was ready, every now and then, to lay down my basket and run for my life, it would have made anyone think I was haunted with an evil conscience, or that I had been lately most terribly frightened; and so, indeed, I had.

However, as I went down thus two or three days, and having seen nothing, I began to be a little bolder, and to think there was really nothing in it but my own imagination; but I could not persuade myself fully of this till I should go down to the shore again, and see this print of a foot and measure it by my own, that I might be assured it was my own foot. But when I came to the place and measured the mark with my own foot, I found my foot not so large by a great deal. This filled my head with new imaginations and gave me the vapors again to the highest degree, so that I shook with cold like one in an ague; and I went home again, filled with the belief that some man or men had been on shore there, that I might be surprised before I was aware; and what course to take for my security I knew not.

O what ridiculous resolutions men take when possessed with fear! The first thing I proposed to myself was to throw down my enclosures and turn all my tame cattle wild into the woods, lest the enemy should find them, and then frequent the island in prospect of like booty; then to dig up my two grainfields, lest they should find grain there, and still be prompted to frequent the island; then to demolish my bower and tent that they might not see any vestiges of habitation, and be prompted to look farther. These were the subject of the first night's cogitations after I was come home again, while the apprehensions which had so over-run my mind were fresh upon me. Thus fear of danger is ten thousand times more terrifying than danger itself.

This confusion of my thoughts kept me awake all night; but in the morning I fell asleep; and having been exhausted in spirit, I slept very soundly and waked much better composed. And now I began to think that this island, which was so exceeding pleasant and fruitful, was not so entirely abandoned as I might imagine; that, although there were no stated inhabitants who lived on the spot, yet that there might sometimes come boats from the mainland either by design or by accident; that I had lived here fifteen years now and had not met with any people yet; and that if at any time they should be driven here, it was probable they soon went away again; and therefore, I had nothing to do but to consider of some safe retreat, in case I should see any savages land.

Now I resolved to make me a second fortification, in the same manner of a semicircle, at a distance from my wall, just where I had planted a double row of trees about twelve years before. These trees having been planted so thick before, wanted but few piles to be driven between them that they might be thicker and stronger, and my wall would be soon finished, so that I had now a double wall, and my outer wall was thickened with pieces of timber, old cables, and everything I could think of to make it strong, having in it seven little holes about as big as I might put my arm out at, through which I contrived to plant my muskets, and fitted them into frames that held them like a carriage, so that I could fire all the seven guns in two minutes' time. This wall I was many a weary month in finishing, and yet never thought myself safe till it was done.

When this was done, I stuck all the ground without my wall, for a great length every way, full with stakes, or sticks, of the osierlike wood, which I found so apt to grow. I believe I set in near twenty thousand of them, leaving a pretty large space between them and my wall, that I might have room to see an enemy, and they might have no shelter from the young trees, if they attempted to approach my outer wall.

Thus, in five years' time I had a wood before my dwelling, growing so monstrous thick and strong that it was perfectly impassable; and no men, of what kind soever, would ever imagine that there was anything beyond it, much less a habitation. As for the way which I proposed to go in and out (for I left no avenue), it was by setting two ladders, one to a part of the rock which was low, and then broke in, and another ladder upon that; so when the two ladders were taken down, no man living could come down to me without doing himself mischief.

৯|(CHAPTER 13 |(৵

ONE day, when wandering more to the west point of the
island than I had ever done yet, and looking out to sea
from a hill, I thought I saw a boat upon the sea, at a great
distance. I looked at it till my eyes were not able to look
any longer. Whether it was a boat or not, I do not know,
but as I descended from the hill to the end of the island,
where, indeed, I had never been before, I was presently
convinced that the seeing the print of a man's foot was not
such a strange thing as I imagined; and, but that it was a
special providence that I was cast upon the side of the
island where the savages never came, I should have known
that canoes from the main, when they happened to be a
little too far out at sea, frequently shot over to that side of
the island for harbor.

When I was come down the hill, I was perfectly confounded and amazed; nor is it possible for me to express

the horror of my mind at seeing the shore spread with skulls, hands, feet, and other bones of human bodies; and, particularly, I observed a place where there had been a fire made and a circle dug in the earth, like a cockpit, where the savage wretches had sat down to their inhuman feastings upon the bodies of their fellow creatures.

I was so astonished with the sight of these things that I entertained no notions of any danger to myself; I turned away my face from the horrid spectacle; my stomach grew sick, and I was just at the point of fainting when Nature discharged the disorder from my stomach. Having vomited, I was a little relieved, but could not bear to stay in the place a moment; so I got me up the hill again with all the speed I could, and I went home to my castle. There I gave God thanks that His special providence had cast me upon that side of the island where the savages never came. They apparently often met and fought in their canoes; and the victors would bring their prisoners over to the west shore, where, according to their dreadful customs, they would kill and eat them. I knew I had been here now almost eighteen years, and might be eighteen years more as entirely concealed as I was now. Yet I entertained such an abhorrence of the savages, and of their wretched inhuman customs, that I kept close within my own plantations for almost two years after this. I did not so much as go to look after my boat all this time, for I could not think of making any more attempts to bring it round the island, lest I should meet with some of these creatures at sea.

Time, however, and the satisfaction I had that I was in no danger of being discovered by these people, began to wear off my uneasiness about them; and I began to live just in the same composed manner as before, only with this difference, that I used more caution and kept my eyes more about me, lest I should happen to be seen by any of them; and particularly, I was more cautious of firing my gun, lest any of them being on the island should happen to hear it. It was therefore a very good providence to me that I had furnished myself with a tame breed of goats, and that I had no need to hunt them anymore. For two years after this, I believe I never fired my gun once off, though I never went out without it; and as I had saved three pistols out of the ship, I always carried two of them out with me, sticking them in my goat's-skin belt. I also furbished up one of the great cutlasses and made me a belt to hang it on; so that I was now a most formidable fellow to look at when I went abroad, if you add to the former description of myself the particular of two pistols and a great broad sword hanging at my side in a belt, but without a scabbard.

Things going on thus for some time, I seemed, excepting these cautions, to be reduced to my former calm sedate way of living. And now I began to think night and day of how I might destroy some of the savages in their cruel, bloody entertainment and, if possible, save the victim they should bring hither to destroy. It would take up a larger volume than this whole work is intended to be, to set down all the contrivances I brooded upon for the destroying these creatures, or at least frightening them so as to prevent their coming hither anymore; but what could one man do among them, when there might be twenty or thirty of them together, with their bows and arrows, with which they could shoot as true to a mark as I could with my gun?

I thought of digging a hole under the place where they made their fire, and putting in five or six pounds of gunpowder, which, when they kindled their fire, would consequently take fire and blow up all that was near it; but as I should be unwilling to waste so much powder upon them, my store being now within the quantity of one barrel, so neither could I be sure of its going off at any certain time, when it might surprise them; and, at best, it would do little more than just blow the fire about their ears and fright them, but not make them forsake the place. So I laid it aside and then proposed that I would place myself in ambush in some convenient place, with my three guns all double-loaded, and, in the middle of their bloody ceremony, let fly at them, when I should be sure to kill or wound perhaps two or three at every shot; and then, falling in upon them with my three pistols and my sword, I made no doubt but that, if there were twenty, I should kill them all.

This fancy pleased my thoughts for weeks, and I often dreamed of it. I went so far with it in my imagination that I employed myself several days to find out proper places to put myself in ambuscade, to watch for them; and at length I found a place in the side of the hill, where I was satisfied I might securely wait till I saw any of their boats coming; and might then, even before they would be ready to come on shore, convey myself, unseen, into some thickets of trees, in one of which there was a hollow large enough to conceal me entirely; and there I might sit and observe all their bloody doings, and take my full aim at their heads, when they were so close together that it would be next to impossible that I could fail wounding three or four of them at the first shot. Accordingly, I loaded two muskets with a brace of slugs each, and four or five smaller bullets, about the size of pistol bullets; and I loaded my fowling piece with near a handful of swan shot of the largest size; I also loaded my pistols with about four bullets each; and in this posture, well provided with ammunition for a second and third charge, I prepared myself for my expedition.

After I had thus laid the scheme of my design, I made my tour every morning up to the top of the hill, which was about three miles from my castle, to see if I could observe any boats coming near the island; but I began to tire of this hard duty, after I had for two or three months not seen the least appearance of any boat on the whole ocean.

As long as I kept my daily lookout, so long also my spirits seemed to be in a suitable form for so outrageous an execution as the killing twenty or thirty naked savages, for an offense which I had not at all entered into a discussion of in my thoughts. But now, when I began to be weary of the fruitless excursion which I had made so far every morning in vain, so my opinion of the action itself began to alter; and I began, with cooler and calmer thoughts, to consider what I was going to engage in. What authority had I to be judge and executioner upon these men as criminals? How far were these people offenders against me, and what right had I to engage in the quarrel of that blood which they shed promiscuously one upon another? How did I know what God Himself judges in this particular case? It is certain these people do not commit this as a crime; they do not know it to be an offense, and then commit it in defiance of divine justice. They think it no more a crime to kill a captive taken in war than we do to kill an ox; nor to eat human flesh than we do to eat mutton.

When I considered this a little, it followed necessarily that these people were not murderers in the sense that I had before condemned them in my thoughts, any more than those Christians were murderers who often put to death the prisoners taken in battle, without giving quarter, though they threw down their arms and submitted. In the next place, it occurred to me that, although the usage they gave one another was brutish and inhuman, yet it was really nothing to me; these people had done me no injury; that if they attempted me, or I saw it necessary for my immediate preservation to fall upon them, something might be said for it; but that I was yet out of their power, and they really had no knowledge of me and consequently no design upon me; and therefore it could not be just for me to fall upon them, unless they first attacked me. I concluded that I ought not to concern myself in this affair; that my business was by all possible means to conceal myself from them, and not to leave the least sign that I was upon the island.

In this disposition I continued for near a year after this; and so far was I from desiring an occasion for falling upon these wretches that I never once went up the hill to see whether there were any of them in sight, or to know whether any had been on shore there or not, that I might not be tempted, by any advantage which might present itself, to fall upon them. Only this I did: I went and removed my boat to the east end of the island, where I ran it into a little cove which I found under some high rocks, and where I knew, by reason of the currents, the savages would not come.

I believe the reader will not think it strange if I confess that the constant dangers I lived in, and the concern that was now upon me, put an end to all invention and to all the contrivances that I had planned for my future conveniences. I had the care of my safety more now upon my hands than that of my food. I cared not to drive a nail or chop a stick of wood, for fear the noise I might make should be heard; much less would I fire a gun, for the same reason. And, above all, I was intolerably uneasy at making any fire, lest the smoke, which is visible at a great distance in the day, should betray me. For this reason I removed

that part of my business which required fire, such as burning of pots and pipes, etc., into a natural cave in the earth,
which, to my unspeakable consolation, I found in the
woods. It went in a vast way, and, I daresay, no savage, had
he been at the mouth of it, would be so hardy as to venture
in; nor, indeed, would any man else, but one who, like me,
wanted nothing so much as a safe retreat.

I discovered this cave by mere accident while I was cutting wood. I was curious to look in it, and getting with difficulty into the mouth of it, I found it was pretty large, that
is to say, sufficient for me to stand upright in it, and perhaps another with me; but I must confess that I made
more haste out than I did in, when, looking farther into
the place, which was perfectly dark, I saw two broad shining eyes of some creature, whether Devil or man I knew
not, which twinkled like two stars, the dim light from the
cave's mouth shining directly in and making the reflection.
However, after some pause, I recovered myself and began
to call myself a thousand fools, and to think that he that
was afraid to see the Devil was not fit to live so many years
in an island all alone; and that I might well think there was
nothing in this cave that was more frightful than myself.
Upon this, plucking up my courage, I took up a firebrand,
and in I rushed again, with the stick flaming in my hand.
I had not gone three steps in but I was almost as much
frightened as I was before; for I heard a very loud sigh, like
that of a man in some pain, and it was followed by a broken noise, as of words half expressed, and then a deep sigh

again. I stepped back, and was indeed struck with such a surprise that it put me into a cold sweat; and if I had had a hat on my head, I will not answer for it that my hair might not have lifted it off. But encouraging myself a little with considering that the power and presence of God was everywhere and was able to protect me, I stepped forward again and, by the light of the firebrand, holding it up a little over my head, I saw lying on the ground a most frightful, old he-goat, just making his will, as we say, and gasping for life, and dying, indeed, of mere old age.

I was now recovered from my surprise and began to look round me. The cave was small, about twelve feet over, but in no manner of shape, neither round nor square, no hands having ever been employed in making it but those of Nature. There was a place at the far side of it that went in further, but was so low that it required me to creep upon my hands and knees to go into it; and I could not do this with my great firebrand, so I gave it over.

The next day I came provided with two large candles of my own making (for I made very good candles now of goat's tallow, using rags or rope yarn for candlewick), and I crept into this low place almost ten yards. When I had got through the strait, I found the roof rose higher up, I believe near twenty feet; and never was such a glorious sight seen in the island, I daresay, as it was to look round the sides and roof of this vault or cave; the walls reflected a hundred thousand lights to me from my two candles. What it was in the rock, whether diamonds or any other precious stones, or gold, which I rather supposed it to be, I knew not. The floor of the grotto was dry and level, and had a sort of a small loose gravel upon it, so that there was no nauseous or venomous creature to be seen, neither was there any damp or wet on the sides or roof; the only difficulty was the entrance; which, however, as it was a place of security and such a retreat as I wanted, I thought that was a convenience; so I rejoiced at the discovery and resolved to bring some of those things which I was most anxious about to this place, particularly my magazine of powder and all my spare arms.

Upon this occasion of removing my ammunition, I opened the barrel of powder which I took up out of the sea, and which had been wet; and I found that the water had penetrated about three or four inches into the powder on every side, which, caking and growing hard, had preserved the inside like a kernel in the shell, so that I had near sixty pounds of very good powder in the center of the cask. This was a very agreeable discovery, so I carried all away thither, never keeping above two or three pounds of powder with me in my castle for fear of a surprise of any kind; I also carried thither all the lead I had left for bullets.

I fancied myself now like one of the ancient giants, which were said to live in caves where none could come at them; for I persuaded myself that if five hundred savages were to hunt me while I was here, they could never find me out; or if they did, they would not venture to attack. The old goat, whom I found expiring, died in the mouth of the cave the next day; and I dug a great hole there, and interred him, to prevent offense to my nose.

I WAS now in the twenty-third year of my residence in this island, and was so naturalized to the place and the manner of living that, could I have but enjoyed the certainty that no savages would come to the place to disturb me, I could have been content to have spent the rest of my time there, even to the last moment, till I had laid me down and died, like the old goat in the cave. I had also arrived to some little amusements, which made the time pass more pleasantly with me than it did before; as, first, I had taught my Poll, as I noted before, to speak; and he did it so familiarly, and talked so plain, that it was very pleasant to me; and he lived with me no less than six and twenty years. My dog was a loving companion to me for no less than sixteen years, and then died of mere old age. As for my cats, they multiplied, and ran wild into the woods, except two or three favorites, which I kept tame, and these were part of my family. Besides these, I always kept two or three household kids about me, which I taught to feed out of my hand; and I had two more parrots, which talked pretty well and would all call "Robin Crusoe," but none like my first; nor, indeed, did I take the pains with any of them that I had done with him. I had also several tame seafowls that I caught upon the shore, and cut their wings; and the stakes which I had planted before my castle wall being now grown up to a good thick grove, these fowls all lived among the low trees and bred there, which was very agreeable to me; so that, as I said above, I began to be very well contented with the life I led, if I could have been secured from the dread of the savages.

But it was otherwise directed; and it may not be amiss for all people who shall meet with my story to make this just observation from it, viz., how frequently the evil which in itself we seek most to shun is oftentimes the very means of our deliverance. I could give many examples of this in the course of my unaccountable life, but in nothing was it more remarkable than in the circumstances of my last years of solitary residence on this island.

❧ CHAPTER 14 ❧

IT WAS now the month of December, in my twenty-third year; and this being the southern solstice (for winter I cannot call it) was the particular time of my harvest, and required my being much abroad in the fields; when going out pretty early in the morning, even before it was thorough daylight, I was surprised with seeing a light of some fire upon the shore, at a distance from me of about two miles, towards the end of the island where I had observed some savages had been; but, to my great affliction, it was on my side of the island.

I was indeed terribly surprised at the sight, and stopped short within my grove, not daring to go out; and yet I had no more peace within, from the apprehensions I had that if these savages, in rambling over the island, should find my corn standing or cut, or any of my works and improvements, they would immediately conclude that there were people in the place, and would never give over till they had found me out. In this extremity, I went back directly to my castle and pulled up the ladder after me.

Then I loaded all my cannon, as I called them, that is to say, my muskets, which were mounted upon my new fortification, and all my pistols, and resolved to defend myself to the last gasp; not forgetting to commend myself to the divine protection, and earnestly to pray to God to deliver me out of the hands of the barbarians. After about two hours, I began to be mighty impatient for intelligence abroad; so, setting up my ladder to the side of the hill and then pulling it up after me, I set it up again and mounted to the top of the hill; and pulling out my perspective glass, which I had taken on purpose, I laid me down flat on my belly on the ground and began to look for the place where I had seen the fire. I presently found there were no less than nine naked savages, sitting round a small fire they had made, not to warm them, for they had no need of that, the weather being extremely hot, but, as I supposed, to dress some of their barbarous diet of human flesh.

They had two canoes with them, which they had hauled up upon the shore; and, as it was then tide of ebb, they seemed to me to wait for the return of the flood, to go away again. It is not easy to imagine what confusion this sight put me into, especially seeing them come on my side of the island, and so near me too; but when I considered their coming must be always with the current of the ebb, I began to be more sedate in my mind, being satisfied that I might go abroad with safety all the time of the tide of flood, if they were not on shore before.

As I expected, so it proved; for as soon as the tide made to the westward, I saw them all take boat and paddle away. I should have observed that for an hour or more before they went off, they went a-dancing; and I could easily discern their postures and gestures by my glass. I could not perceive, by my nicest observation, but that they had not the least covering upon them.

As soon as I saw them shipped and gone, I took two guns upon my shoulders, and two pistols in my girdle, and my great sword by my side and, with all the speed I was able to make, went away to the place where I had discovered the savages; and as soon as I got thither, which was not in less than two hours (for I could not go apace, being so loaden with arms), I could see the marks of horror which the dismal work they had been about had left behind it, viz., the blood, the bones, and part of the flesh of human bodies, eaten and devoured by those wretches with merriment and sport. I was so filled with indignation at the sight that I now began to premeditate the destruction of the next that I saw there, let them be whom or how many soever.

It seemed evident to me that the visits which they made thus to this island were not very frequent, for it was above fifteen months before any more of them came on shore there again; that is to say, I neither saw them, nor any footsteps or signs of them; yet all this while I lived uncomfortably, by reason of the constant apprehensions of their coming upon me by surprise; from whence I observe that the expectation of evil is more bitter than the suffering, especially if there is no room to shake off that expectation.

During this time I was in the murdering humor, and took up most of my hours, which should have been better employed, in contriving how to fall upon the savages the very next time I should see them; nor did I consider at all that, if I killed one party, suppose ten or a dozen, I was still the next day, or week, or month, to kill another, and so another, even ad infinitum, till I should be at length no less a murderer than they were in being man-eaters, and perhaps much more so. I spent my days now in great anxiety of mind; and if I did at any time venture abroad, it was not without looking round me with the greatest care and caution imaginable. And now I found, to my great comfort, how happy it was that I provided for a tame flock or herd of goats; for I durst not, upon any account, fire my gun, especially near the side of that island where they usually came, lest I should alarm the savages; and if they had fled from me now, I was sure to have them come again, with perhaps two or three hundred canoes with them, in a few days, and then I knew what to expect. However, I wore out a year and three months more before I ever saw any more of the savages.

The perturbation of my mind, during this fifteen months' interval, was very great: I slept unquiet, dreamed always frightful dreams, and often started out of my sleep in the night; in the day, great troubles overwhelmed my mind—But to waive all this for a while. It was in the middle of May, on the sixteenth day, I think, that it blew a very great storm of wind all day, with a great deal of lightning and thunder, and a very foul night it was after it. As I was reading in the Bible, and taken up with very serious thoughts about my present condition, I was surprised with the noise of a gun, as I thought, fired at sea. This was a surprise quite of a different nature from any I had met with before; for the notions this put into my thoughts were quite of another kind. I started up in the greatest haste imaginable and, in a trice, clapped my ladder to the middle place of the rock and pulled it after me; and, mounting it the second time, got to the top of the hill the very moment that a flash of fire bid me listen for a second gun, which, in about half a minute, I heard; and, by the sound, knew that it was from that part of the sea where I was driven down the current in my boat.

I immediately considered that this must be some ship in distress, and that they had some comrade or some other ship in company, and fired these guns for signals to obtain help. I had the presence of mind, at that minute, to think that, though I could not help them, it might be they might help me; so I brought together all the dry wood I could get at hand, and making a handsome pile, I set it on fire upon the hill. It burned so well that I was certain, if there was any such thing as a ship, they must needs see it; and no doubt they did; for as soon as ever my fire blazed up, I heard another gun, and after that several others, all from the same quarter. I plied my fire all night long, till day-break; when I saw something at a great distance at sea, full east of the island, whether a sail or a hull I could not then distinguish, as the weather was something hazy.

I looked frequently at it all that day, and soon perceived that it did not move; so I presently concluded that it was a ship at anchor; and being eager, you may be sure, to be satisfied, I took my gun in my hand and ran towards the south side of the island to the rocks where I had formerly been carried away with the current; and getting up there, the weather by this time being perfectly clear, I could plainly see, to my great sorrow, the wreck of a ship cast away in the night upon those concealed rocks which made a kind of counter-stream, or eddy, and were the occasion of my recovering from the most desperate, hopeless condition that ever I had been in in all my life. Thus, what is one man's safety is another man's destruction; for it seems these men, whoever they were, being out of their knowledge, and the rocks being wholly underwater, had been driven upon them in the night. Their firing off guns for help, especially when they saw, as I imagined, my fire, filled me with many thoughts. First, I imagined that, upon seeing my light, they might have put themselves into their boat and endeavored to make the shore; but that the sea going very high, they might have been cast away; other times I imagined they had some other ship or ships in company, who, upon the signals of distress they had made, had taken them up and carried them off.

As all these were but conjectures at best, so, in the condition I was in, I could do no more than look upon the misery of the poor men and pity them; which had still this good effect on my side that it gave me more and more cause to give thanks to God, who had so happily and comfortably provided for me in my desolate condition; and that, of two ships' companies who were now cast away upon this part of the world, not one life should be spared but mine. I cannot explain what a strange longing I felt in my soul upon sight of that wreck, breaking out sometimes thus: "O that there had been but one soul saved out of this ship, to have escaped to me, that I might have had one companion, one fellow creature to have spoken to me, and to have conversed with!" In all the time of my solitary life, I never felt so earnest, so strong a desire after the society of my fellow creatures, or so deep a regret at the want of it.

I BELIEVE I repeated the words, "O that it had been but one!" a thousand times; and when I spoke the words my hands would clinch together, and my fingers would press my palms so that if I had had any soft thing in my hand, it would have crushed it involuntarily. But it was not to be; either their fate or mine, or both, forbade it; and I had only the affliction, some days after, to see the corpse of a drowned boy come on shore at the end of the island which was next the shipwreck. He had no clothes on but a seaman's waistcoat, a pair of linen drawers and a blue linen shirt, nothing to direct me so much as to guess what nation he was of. He had nothing in his pockets but two pieces of eight and a tobacco pipe; the last was to me of ten times more value than the first.

It was now calm, and I had a great mind to venture out in my boat to this wreck, not doubting but I might find something on board that might be useful to me, or that there might be yet some living creature on board whose life I might save. I hastened back to my castle, prepared everything for my voyage, took a quantity of bread, a great pot of fresh water, a compass to steer by, a bottle of rum, and a basket of raisins; and thus loading myself with everything necessary, I went down to my boat, got her afloat, loaded all my cargo in her, and then went home again for more. My second cargo was a great bag of rice, the umbrella to set up over my head for a shade, another large pot of fresh water, and about two dozen of my small loaves, or barley cakes, with a bottle of goat's milk and a cheese, all which, with great labor and sweat, I carried to my boat.

Next morning, I launched out with the first of the tide; and praying to God to direct my voyage, I went at a great rate directly for the wreck, and in less than two hours I came up to it. It was a dismal sight to look at: the ship, which, by its building, was Spanish, stuck fast, jammed in between two rocks; all her stern and quarter were beaten to pieces with the sea; her mainmast and foremast were broken short off; but her head and bow appeared firm. When I came close to her, a dog appeared upon her, who, seeing me coming, yelped and cried; and as soon as I called him, jumped into the sea to come to me. I took him into the boat, but found him almost dead with hunger and thirst. I gave him a cake of my bread, and he devoured it like a ravenous wolf that had been starving a fortnight in the snow. I then gave the poor creature some fresh water, with which, if I would have let him, he would have burst himself. After this, I went on board. The first sight I met with was two men drowned in the forecastle, with their arms fast about one another. I concluded that when the ship struck, it being in a storm, the sea broke so high, and so continually over her, that the men were strangled with the constant rushing in of the water.

Besides the dog, there was nothing left in the ship that had life; nor any goods that I could see, but what were spoiled by the water. I saw several seamen's chests, and I got two of them into the boat without examining what was in them. I found, besides, a cask full of liquor, of about twenty gallons, which I got into my boat with much difficulty. There was a powder horn, with about four pounds of powder in it, and I took it. I took a fire shovel and tongs, which I wanted extremely; as also two little brass kettles, a copper pot and a gridiron. With this cargo, and the dog, I came away, the tide beginning to make home again; and the same evening, I reached the island, weary to the last degree.

I reposed that night in the boat; and in the morning I resolved to harbor what I had got in my new cave. After refreshing myself, I got all my cargo on shore and began to examine the particulars. The cask of liquor I found to be a kind of rum. In one of the chests I found a fine case of bottles filled with cordial waters. I found two pots of very good sweetmeats, so fastened on the top that the salt water had not hurt them. I found some shirts, which were very welcome to me; and about a dozen and a half of white linen handkerchiefs and colored neckcloths; the former were also very welcome, being exceeding refreshing to wipe my face in a hot day. Besides this, I found three great bags of pieces of eight, which held about eleven hundred in all; and in one of them, wrapped up in a paper, six doubloons of gold and some small bars or wedges of gold. In the other chest were some clothes, but of little value. Upon the whole, I got very little that was of any use to me; for, as to the money, it was as the dirt under my feet; and I would have given it all for three or four pair of English shoes and stockings, which I greatly wanted, but had none on my feet for many years. I had indeed got two pair of shoes, which I took off the feet of the two drowned men, and I found two pair more in one of the chests; but they were not like our English shoes, either for ease or service, being rather what we call pumps.

Having now brought all my things on shore and secured them, I went back to my boat and paddled her along the shore to her old harbor, where I laid her up, and made the best of my way to my old habitation, where I found every-thing safe and quiet. I began now to repose myself, live after my old fashion, and take care of my family affairs; and for a while, I lived easy enough, only that I was more vigilant than I used to be, looked out oftener, and did not go abroad so much; and if at any time I did stir with any freedom, it was always to the east part of the island, where I was pretty well satisfied the savages never came.

IT WAS one of the nights in the rainy season in March, the four and twentieth year of my first setting foot in this island of solitude, I was lying in my hammock, awake; very well in health, had no pain, no distemper, no uneasi-ness of body, nor any uneasiness of mind, more than ordi-nary, but could by no means close my eyes to sleep. It is impossible to set down the innumerable thoughts that whirled through that great thoroughfare of the brain, the memory, in this night's time; I ran over the whole history of my life to my coming to this island. I looked back upon the excellent advice of my father, the opposition to which was, as I may call it, my *original sin*, my subsequent mistakes of the same kind having been the means of my coming into this miserable condition; for had I been con-tented to have gone on gradually, I might have been by this time one of the most considerable planters in the Brazils. In my reflections upon my state since I came on shore, I compared the happy posture of my affairs in the first years of my habitation here to the life of anxiety, fear, and care which I had lived in ever since I had seen the print of a foot in the sand; not that I did not believe the savages had frequented the island all the while, but I had never known it, and was as happy in not knowing my danger as if I had never really been exposed to it. This furnished my thoughts with this reflection: How infinitely good that Providence is, which has provided, in its government of mankind, such narrow bounds to his sight and knowledge! Though he walks in the midst of many thousand dangers, the sight of which, if discovered to him, would distract his mind and sink his spirits, he is kept serene and calm by having these dangers hid from his eyes.

I came to reflect seriously upon the real danger I had been in for so many years in this very island, and how I had walked about with all possible tranquillity, even when perhaps nothing but the brow of a hill, a great tree, or the casual approach of night had been between me and the worst kind of destruction, viz., that of falling into the hands of cannibals, who would have seized on me with the same view as I would on a goat, and have thought it no more a crime to kill and devour me than I did a pigeon. I was sincerely thankful to my Preserver, to whose protection I acknowledged with great humility all these unknown deliverances were due.

When these thoughts were over, it occurred to me to inquire from how far off the coast these savages came, and why I might not be as able to go over thither as they were to come to me. I never so much as troubled myself to consider what I should do with myself when I went thither, or what would become of me if I fell into the hands of the savages, my mind being wholly bent upon the notion of my passing over in my boat to the mainland. There I might perhaps meet with relief, or I might coast along, as I did on the African shore, till I came to some inhabited country; and, perhaps, I might fall in with some Christian ship that might take me in; and, if the worst came to the worst, I could but die, which would put an end to all my miseries at once. Pray note, all this was the fruit of a disturbed mind, an impatient temper, made desperate by the long continuance of my troubles, and the disappointments I had met in the wreck, where I had been so near obtaining what I so earnestly longed for, viz., somebody to speak to, and to learn some knowledge from them of the place where I was, and of the probable means of my deliverance. All my calm of mind, in my resignation to Providence, and waiting the issue of the dispositions of Heaven, seemed to be suspended; and I had, as it were, no power to turn my thoughts to anything but to the project of a voyage to the main, which came upon me with such force, and such an impetuosity of desire, that it was not to be resisted.

When this had agitated my thoughts for two hours or more, Nature threw me into a sound sleep. I dreamed that I saw upon the shore two canoes and eleven savages, and that they brought with them another savage, whom they were going to kill in order to eat him; when, on a sudden, the savage they were going to kill jumped away and ran for his life; and I dreamed that he came running into my little thick grove before my fortification to hide; and that I showed myself to him and, smiling upon him, encouraged him; that he kneeled down to me, seeming to pray me to assist him; upon which I made him go up my ladder and carried him into my cave, and he became my servant; and that I said to myself, Now I may certainly venture to the mainland; for this fellow will serve me as a pilot, and will tell whither to go for provisions, and whither not to go for fear of being devoured. I waked with this thought and was under such inexpressible impressions of joy at the prospect of *my* escape in my dream that the disappointments which I felt upon coming to myself, and finding that it was no more than a dream, threw me into a very great dejection of spirits.

Upon this, however, I made this conclusion: that my only way to attempt an escape was to get a savage into my possession; and, if possible, it should be one of their prisoners whom they should bring hither to kill. But these thoughts were attended with this difficulty that it was impossible to effect this without attacking a whole caravan of them and killing them all; and this was not only a desperate attempt, and might miscarry; but my heart trembled at the thought of shedding so much blood, though it was for my deliverance. However, at last, after many secret disputes with myself, the eager desire of deliverance prevailed, and I resolved to get one of those savages into my hands, cost what it would. My next thing was to contrive how to do it; but as I could pitch upon no probable means for it, so I resolved to put myself upon the watch, to see them when they came on shore, and leave the rest to the event, taking such measures as thc opportunity should present.

With these resolutions, I set myself upon the scout as often as possible, and indeed so often that I was heartily tired of it; for it was above a year and a half that I waited, but no canoes appeared.

❧ CHAPTER 15 ❧

I WAS at last surprised, one morning early, with seeing no less than five canoes all on shore together on my side the island, and the people who belonged to them all landed and out of my sight. Knowing that they always came four or more in a boat, I could not tell how to take my measures, to attack twenty or thirty men singlehanded, so I lay still in my castle, perplexed and discomforted. However, I put myself into all the postures for an attack that I had formerly provided, and was ready for action. At length, being very impatient, I set my guns at the foot of my ladder and clambered up to the top of the hill. Standing so that my head did not appear above the hill, I observed, by the help of my perspective glass, that they were no less than thirty in number, that they had a fire kindled and that they had meat dressed and were dancing, with I know not how many barbarous gestures, round the fire.

While I was thus looking on them, I perceived two miserable wretches dragged from the boats, where, it seems, they were laid by, and were now brought out for the slaughter. I saw one of them being knocked down with a club, and two or three others were at work immediately cutting him open for their cookery, while the other victim was left standing by himself till they should be ready for him. In that very moment, this poor wretch, seeing himself a little at liberty and unbound, Nature inspired him with hopes of life, and he started away from them and ran with incredible swiftness along the sands, directly towards that part of the coast where my habitation was. I was dreadfully frightened, I must acknowledge, when I perceived him run my way, and especially when, as I thought, I saw him pursued by the whole body; and now I expected that part of my dream was coming to pass, and that he would certainly take shelter in my grove. However, I kept my station, and my spirits began to recover when I found that there was not above three men that followed him; and still more was I encouraged when I found that he outstripped them exceedingly in running.

There was between them and my castle the creek, where I landed my cargoes out of the ship; and this he must swim over, or the poor wretch would be taken there; but when he came thither, he swam through in about thirty strokes, landed, and ran on with exceeding strength and swiftness. When his three pursuers came to the creek, I found that two of them could swim, but the third could not, and he looked at the others and then went softly back to the fire. I observed that the two who swam were yet more than twice as long swimming over the creek as the fellow was that fled from them. It came now irresistibly upon my thoughts that now was the time to get me a servant, and perhaps a companion or assistant, and that I was called plainly by Providence to save this poor creature's life. I immediately ran down the ladders, fetched my two guns, and getting up again with haste to the top of the hill, I crossed toward the sea and, having a very short cut, and all downhill, placed myself in the way between the pursuers and the pursued, hallooing aloud to him that fled, who, looking back, was at first, perhaps, as much frightened at me as at them. But I beckoned with my hand to him to come back; and, in the meantime, I slowly advanced towards the two that followed. Then, rushing upon the foremost, I knocked him down and stunned him with the stock of my piece. The other who pursued him stopped, as if he had been frightened, and I advanced apace towards him; but as I came nearer, I perceived he had a bow and arrow, and was fitting it to shoot at me; so I was necessitated to shoot at him first, which I did, and killed him at the first shot.

The poor savage who fled but had stopped, though he saw both his enemies fallen, yet was so frightened with the fire and noise of my piece that he stood stock-still. I hallooed again to him and made signs to come forward, which he understood, and came a little way, then stopped again; and I could then perceive that he stood trembling, as if he had been taken prisoner and was to be killed. I beckoned to him again to come to me and gave him all the signs of encouragement that I could think of; and he came nearer and nearer, kneeling down every ten or twelve steps, in token of acknowledgment for saving his life. I smiled at him and looked pleasantly, and beckoned to him to come still nearer; at length he came close to me, kneeled down again, kissed the ground, and laid his head upon the ground, and taking me by the foot, set my foot upon his head; this, it seems, was in token of swearing to be my slave forever. I took him up, and made much of him.

But there was more work to do yet, for I perceived the savage whom I knocked down began to come to himself; so I pointed to him and showed him the savage, that he was not dead; upon this he spoke some words to me, and though I could not understand them, yet they were pleasant to hear; for they were the first sound of a man's voice that I had heard, my own excepted, for above twenty-five years. The savage who was knocked down recovered himself so far as to sit up upon the ground, and I perceived that my savage began to be afraid; but when I saw that, I presented my other piece at the man, as if I would shoot him. Upon this my savage, for so I call him now, made a motion to me to lend him my sword which hung naked in a belt by my side. He no sooner had it but he ran to his enemy, and at one blow cut off his head so cleverly no executioner could have done it better. Then he came laughing to me, in sign of triumph, and with abundance of gestures, which I did not understand, laid the sword down, with the head of the savage that he had killed, just before me.

But that which astonished him most was to know how I killed the other Indian so far off; so, pointing to him, he made signs to me to let him go to him; so I bade him go, as well as I could. When he came to him, he stood like one amazed, looking at him, turning him first on one side, then on the other, looked at the wound the bullet had made in his breast, where no great quantity of blood had followed, for he had bled inwardly. He took up his bow and arrows, and came back; so I turned to go away, and beckoned him to follow me, making signs to him that more might come after them. Upon this, he made signs to me that he should bury them with sand, that they might not be seen by the rest, if they followed; and so I made signs to him again, to do so. He fell to work; and, in an instant, he had scraped a hole in the sand with his hands, big enough to bury the first in, and then dragged him into it and covered him; and did so by the other also; I believe he had buried them both in a quarter of an hour. Then calling him away, I carried him, not to my castle, but to my cave on the farther part of the island; so I did not let my dream come to pass in that part, viz., that he came into my grove for shelter. Here I gave him bread and a bunch of raisins to eat and water; and, having refreshed him, I showed him a place where I had laid some rice straw, and a blanket upon it, which I used to sleep upon myself sometimes, so the poor creature lay down and went to sleep.

He was a comely, handsome fellow, perfectly well made, with straight, strong limbs, not too large, tall and well shaped, and, as I reckoned, about twenty-six years of age. He had a good countenance, not a fierce and surly aspect, but seemed to have something very manly in his face; and yet he had all the sweetness and softness of a European in his countenance too, especially when he smiled. His hair was long and black, his forehead very high and large, and a great vivacity and sparkling sharpness in his eyes. His skin was a bright kind of dun-olive color. His face was round and plump; his nose small, a good mouth, thin lips, and fine teeth well set, white as ivory.

After he had slumbered about half an hour, he awoke and came out of the cave to me, for I had been milking my goats, which I had in the enclosure just by. When he espied me, he came running to me, laying himself down again upon the ground, with all the possible signs of a humble, thankful disposition, making a great many antic gestures to show it. At last, he laid his head flat upon the ground, close to my foot, and set my other foot upon his head, as he had done before; and after this made all the signs to me of subjection, servitude and submission imaginable, to let me know how he would serve me as long as he lived; and I let him know I was very well pleased with him.

In a little time I began to speak to him and teach him to speak to me; and, first, I let him know his name should be Friday, which was the day I saved his life. I likewise taught him to say Master, and then let him know that was to be my name. I taught him to say yes and no, and to know the meaning of them. I gave him some milk in an earthen pot, and let him see me drink it before him, and sop my bread in it; and gave him a cake of bread to do the like, which he quickly complied with, and made signs that it was very good. I kept there with him all that night; but as soon as it was day, I beckoned to him to come with me, and let him know I would give him some clothes; at which he seemed very glad, for he was stark naked. As we went by the place where he had buried the two men, he pointed exactly to the place, and showed me the marks that he had made to find them again, making signs to me that we should dig them up and eat them. At this I appeared very angry, expressed my abhorrence of it, made as if I would vomit at the thoughts of it, and beckoned with my hand to him to come away, which he did, with great submission. I then led him up to the top of the hill to see if his enemies were gone; and pulling out my glass, I looked, and saw plainly the place where they had been, but no appearance of them or their canoes.

Having now more courage, and consequently more

curiosity, I took my man Friday with me, giving him the sword in his hand, with the bow and arrows at his back, which I found he could use very dexterously, making him carry one gun for me, and I two for myself; and away we marched to the place where these creatures had been, for I had a mind now to get fuller intelligence of them. When I came to the place, my very blood ran chill in my veins; and my heart sunk within me at the horror of the spectacle, though Friday made nothing of it. The place was covered with human bones, the ground dyed with their blood, and great pieces of flesh left here and there, half-eaten, mangled, and scorched; all the tokens of the triumphant feast they had been making there, after a victory over their enemies. Friday, by his signs, made me understand that they had brought over four prisoners to feast upon; that three of them were eaten up, and that he, pointing to himself, was the fourth; that there had been a great battle between them and a neighboring king, whose subjects he had been one of, and that they had taken a great number of prisoners, all which were carried to several places by those who had taken them in the fight, in order to feast upon them, as was done here.

I caused Friday to gather up all the skulls, bones, flesh, and whatever remained, and lay them together in a heap, and make a great fire upon it, and burn them all to ashes. I found Friday had still a hankering after some of the flesh, and was still a cannibal in his nature; but I showed so much abhorrence at the least appearance of it that he durst not eat, for I had let him know that I would kill him if he did.

We then came back to our castle; and there I gave my man Friday a pair of linen drawers, which I had out of one of the chests I found in the wreck and which, with a little alteration, fitted him very well; and then I made him a jerkin of goat's skin, as well as my skill would allow (for I was now grown a tolerable good tailor); and I gave him a cap, which I made of hare's skin, very convenient and fashionable enough; and thus he was clothed, and was mighty well pleased to see himself almost as well clothed as his master. It is true, he went awkwardly in those clothes at first, but after a little easing them where he complained they hurt him, and using himself to them, he took to them very well.

The next day I began to consider where I should lodge him; and that I might do well for him, and yet be perfectly easy myself, I made a little tent for him in the vacant place between my two fortifications, in the inside of the last and in the outside of the first. As there was an entrance there into my cave, I made a formal framed doorcase and a door to it of boards and set it up in the passage, a little within the entrance; and causing the door to open in the inside, I barred it up in the night, taking in my ladders too; so that Friday could no way come at me in the inside of my innermost wall without waking me; for my first wall had now a complete roof over it of long poles, covering all my tent, and leaning up to the side of the hill, which was again laid across with smaller sticks, and then thatched over with rice straw; and at the hole which was left to go in or out by the ladder, I had placed a kind of trapdoor, which, if it had been attempted on the outside, would have fallen down and made a great noise; as to weapons, I took them all in to my side every night. But I needed none of all this precaution, for never man had a more faithful, loving, sincere servant than Friday was to me—his very affections were tied to me, like those of a child to a father; and I daresay he would have sacrificed his life for mine upon any occasion whatsoever; the many testimonies he gave me of this soon convinced me that I needed to use no precautions as to my safety on his account.

This frequently gave me occasion to observe, and that with wonder, that it has pleased God, in His providence, to bestow upon all His creatures the same powers, the same reason, the same affections, the same sentiments of kindness and obligation, the same passions and resentments of wrongs, the same sense of gratitude, sincerity, fidelity, and all the capacities of doing good that He has given to us; and that when He offers them occasions of exerting these, they are as ready, nay, more ready, to apply them to the right uses for which they were bestowed than we are.

I was greatly delighted with my new companion and made it my business to teach him everything that was proper to make him handy and helpful; but especially to make him speak and understand me when I spoke; and he was the aptest scholar that ever was; and particularly was so merry, so constantly diligent, and so pleased when he could but understand me, or make me understand him, that it was very pleasant to me to talk to him. Now my life began to be so easy that I began to say to myself that could I but have been safe from more savages, I cared not if I was never to remove from the place where I lived.

16

to let him taste of other flesh;

❧ CHAPTER 16 ❦

AFTER I had been two or three days returned to my castle, I thought that, in order to bring Friday off from his horrid way of feeding, and from the relish of a cannibal's stomach, I ought to let him taste of other flesh; so I took him out with me one morning to the woods. I went, indeed, intending to kill a kid out of my own flock, and bring it home and dress it; but as I was going, I saw a she-goat lying down in the shade, and two young kids sitting by her. I catched hold of Friday. "Hold," said I, "stand still"; and made signs to him not to stir. Immediately I presented my piece, shot, and killed one of the kids. Poor Friday, who had, at a distance, seen me kill the savage, his enemy, but could not imagine how it was done, trembled and shook, and looked so amazed that I thought he would have sunk down. He did not see the kid I had killed, but ripped up his waistcoat to feel whether he was wounded and, as I found presently, thought I was resolved to kill him; for he came and kneeled down to me and, embracing my knees, said a great many things I did not understand; but I could easily see the meaning was to pray me not to kill him.

Taking him up by the hand, I laughed at him and, pointing to the kid which I had killed, beckoned to him to run and fetch it, which he did; and while he was wondering, and looking to see how the creature was killed, I loaded my gun again. By and by, I saw a great parrot sitting upon a tree, within shot; so, to let Friday understand a little what I would do, I called him to me again; and pointing to the parrot, to my gun, and to the ground under the parrot, I made him understand that I would shoot and kill that bird; accordingly I fired and bade him look, and immediately he saw the parrot fall. He stood like one frightened again, notwithstanding all I had said to him; and I found he was the more amazed because he did not see me put anything into the gun, but thought that there must be some wonderful fund of death and destruction in that thing, able to kill anything near or far off; and the astonishment this created in him was such as could not wear off for a long time; and I believe, if I would have let him, he would have worshiped me and my gun. As for the gun itself, he would not touch it for several days after; but he would speak to it and talk to it, as if it had answered him, when he was by himself; which, as I afterwards learned of him, was to desire it not to kill him.

Well, I brought home the kid, and I took the skin off,

and cut it out as well as I could; and I boiled some of the flesh in a pot and made some broth. I gave some to my man, who liked it very well; but that which was strangest to him was to see me eat salt with it. He made a sign to me that the salt was not good to eat; and putting a little into his mouth, he would spit and sputter at it; on the other hand, I took some meat into my mouth without salt, and I pretended to spit and sputter for want of salt, as fast as he had done at the salt; but he would never care for salt with his meat or in his broth.

Having thus fed him with boiled meat and broth, I was resolved to feast him the next day with roasting a piece of kid; this I did by hanging it before the fire on a string, as I had seen many people do in England, setting two poles up, one on each side of the fire, and one across on the top, and tying the string to the cross stick, letting the meat turn continually. This Friday admired very much; and when he came to taste the flesh, he took so many ways to tell me how well he liked it that I could not but understand him; and at last he told me, as well as he could, he would never eat man's flesh anymore, which I was very glad to hear.

I set him to work to beating some grain out, and sifting it in the manner I used to do; and he soon understood how to do it as well as I, especially after he had seen what the meaning of it was, and that it was to make bread of; for after that, I let him see me make my bread, and bake it too; and in a little time Friday was able to do all this work for me, as well as I could do it myself.

I began now to consider that, having two mouths to feed instead of one, I must provide more ground for my harvest, and plant a larger quantity of grain than I used to do; so I marked out a larger piece of land, and began the fence in the same manner as before, in which Friday worked not only willingly and hard but very cheerfully. And I told him what it was for; that it was for grain to make more bread because he was now with me, and that I might have enough for him and myself too. He appeared very sensible of that part, and let me know that he thought I had much more labor upon me on his account than I had for myself, and that he would work the harder for me if I would tell him what to do.

This was the pleasantest year of all the life I led in this place. Friday began to talk pretty well, and understand the names of almost everything I had occasion to call for and of every place I had to send him to, and talked a great deal to me; so that I began now to have some use for my tongue again, which, indeed, I had very little occasion for before, that is to say, about speech. Besides the pleasure of talking to him, I had a singular satisfaction in the fellow himself: his simple, unfeigned honesty appeared to me more and more every day, and I began really to love him; and, on his side, I believe he loved me more than it was possible for him ever to love anything before.

I had a mind once to try if he had any hankering inclination to his own country again; and having taught him English so well that he could answer me almost any question, I asked him whether the nation that he belonged to never conquered in battle. At which he smiled, and said, "Yes, yes, we always fight the better"; and so we began the following discourse:

MASTER. You always fight the better? How come you to be taken prisoner then, Friday?

FRIDAY. My nation beat much, for all that.

MASTER. How beat? If your nation beat them, how come you to be taken?

FRIDAY. They more many than my nation in the place where me was; they take one, two, three, and me; my nation overbeat them in the yonder place, where me no was; there my nation take one, two, great thousand.

MASTER. But why did not your side recover you from the hands of your enemies, then?

FRIDAY. They run one, two, three, and me, and make go in the canoe; my nation have no canoe that time.

MASTER. Well, Friday, and what does your nation do with the men they take? Do they carry them away and eat them, as these did?

FRIDAY. Yes, my nation eat mans too; eat all up.

MASTER. Where do they carry them?

FRIDAY. Go to other place, where they think.

MASTER. Do they come hither?

FRIDAY. Yes, yes, they come hither; come other else place.

MASTER. Have you been here with them?

FRIDAY. Yes, I have been here. (Points to the northwest side of the island, which, it seems, was their side.)

Some time after, when I took the courage to carry him to that side, he knew the place, and told me he was there once when they ate up twenty men, two women, and one child; he could not tell twenty in English, but he numbered them by laying so many stones in a row, and pointing to me to tell them over.

I asked him how far it was from our island to the mainland and whether the canoes were not often lost. He told me there no canoes were ever lost; but that, after a little way out to sea, there was a current, always one way in the morning, the other in the afternoon. This I understood afterwards was occasioned by the great draft and reflux of the mighty river Orinoco, in the mouth of which our island lay; and that land which I perceived to the west and northwest was the great island Trinidad, on the north point of the mouth of the river. I asked Friday a thousand questions about the country, the inhabitants, the sea, the coast, and what nations were near. He told me all he knew, with the greatest openness imaginable. I asked him the names of the several nations of his sort of people, but could get no other name than Caribs; from whence I understood that these were the Caribbees, which our maps place on the part of America which reaches from the mouth of the Orinoco to Guiana, and onwards to St. Martha. He told me that up a great way beyond the setting of the moon, which must be west from their country, there dwelt white, bearded men like me, and pointed to my great whiskers; and that they had killed much "mans," by which I understood he meant the Spaniards. I inquired if he could tell me how I might go from this island and get among those white men; he told me, "Yes, yes, you may go in two canoe." I could not understand what he meant till, at last, with great difficulty, I found he meant it must be in a large boat, as big as two canoes. From this time I entertained some hopes that, one time or other, I might find an opportunity to make my escape from this place, and that this poor savage might be a means to help me.

DURING that long time that Friday had now been with me, and that he began to speak to me and understand me, I was not wanting to lay a foundation of religious knowledge in his mind; particularly I asked him, one time, who made him? The poor creature thought I had asked him who was his father; but I took it up by another handle and asked him who made the sea, the ground we walked on, and the hills and woods. He told me it was one old Benamuckee that lived in the great mountains; he could describe nothing of this person but that he was very old, much older, he said, than the sea or the land, than the moon or the stars. I asked him then, if this old person had made all things, why did not all things worship him? He looked very grave, and with perfect innocence said, "All things say 'O!' to him." I asked him if the people who die in his country went away anywhere. He said, yes; they all went to Benamuckee. Then I asked him whether these they ate up went thither too. He said, "Yes."

From these things I began to instruct him in the knowledge of the true God: I told him that the great Maker of all things lived up there, pointing up towards heaven; that He governed the world by the same power and providence by which He made it; that He was omnipotent, and could do everything for us, give everything to us, take everything from us. He listened with great attention, and received with pleasure the notion of Jesus Christ being sent to redeem us, and of the manner of making our prayers to God, and His being able to hear us, even in heaven. He told me that, if our God could hear us up beyond the sun, He must needs be a greater God than their Benamuckee, who lived but a little way off, and yet could not hear till they went up to the mountains where he dwelt to speak to him.

I had, God knows, more sincerity than knowledge in the methods I took for this poor creature's instruction, and in laying things open to him I instructed myself in many things that I had not fully considered before, but which occurred naturally to my mind upon searching into them for his information; and I had more affection in my inquiry after things upon this occasion than ever I felt before, so that, whether this poor wild wretch was the better for me or no, I had great reason to be thankful that ever he came to me. My grief sat lighter upon me; my habitation grew comfortable to me beyond measure; and when I reflected that in this solitary life which I had been confined to, I had not only been moved to look up to Heaven myself, and to seek the hand that had brought me here, but was now to be made an instrument, under Providence, to save the life, and, for aught I knew, the soul, of a poor savage, and bring him to the true knowledge of the Christian doctrine; I say, when I reflected upon these things, a secret joy ran through every part of my soul.

❧ CHAPTER 17 ❧

AFTER Friday and I became more intimately acquainted, and that he could understand almost all I said to him, and speak pretty fluently, though in broken English, to me, I acquainted him with my own history, or at least so much of it as related to my coming to this place: how I had lived here and how long. I let him into the mystery, for such it was to him, of gunpowder and bullet, and taught him to shoot. I gave him a knife, which he was wonderfully delighted with; and I made him a belt in which he carried a hatchet.

I described to him the country of England, which I came from; how we lived, how we worshiped God, how we behaved to one another; and how we traded in ships to all parts of the world. I gave him an account of the wreck which I had been on board of, and showed him, as near as I could, the place where she lay; but she was all beaten in pieces before, and gone. I showed him the ruins of our boat, which we lost when we escaped, and which I could not stir with my whole strength then; but was now fallen almost all to pieces. Upon seeing this boat, Friday stood musing a great while, and said nothing. I asked him what it was he studied upon. At last, says he, "Me see such boat like come to place at my nation." I did not understand him a good while; but, at last, when I had examined farther into it, I understood that a boat, such as that had been, came on shore upon the country where he lived; that is, it was driven thither by stress of weather. I presently imagined that some European ship must have been cast away upon their coast, and the boat might have gotten loose and driven ashore; so I inquired after a description of the boat.

Friday described the boat to me well enough; and he added, with some warmth, "We save the white mans from drown." I asked him how many? He told upon his fingers seventeen. I asked him then what became of them? He told me, "They live, they dwell at my nation."

This put new thoughts into my head; for I imagined that these might be the men belonging to the ship that was cast away in the sight of my island; and who, after the ship was struck on the rock, had saved themselves in their boat, and were landed upon that wild shore among the savages. Upon this, I inquired of him more critically what was become of them; he assured me that they had been there about four years, that the savages let them alone and gave them victuals to live on. I asked him how it came to pass they did not kill them and eat them? He said, "No, they make brother with them"; and then he added, "They no eat mans but when make the war fight"; that is to say, they never eat any men but such as come to fight with them, and are taken in battle.

It was after this some considerable time that being upon the top of the hill, from whence I had, in a clear day, discovered the main or continent of America, Friday, the weather being very serene, looks very earnestly towards the mainland, and in a kind of surprise falls a-jumping and dancing, and calls out to me, "O joy! O glad! There see my country, there my nation!" I observed an extraordinary sense of eagerness in his face, and his eyes sparkled, as if he had a mind to be in his own country again. This observation put a great many thoughts into me, which made me at first not so easy about my man Friday as I was before; and I made no doubt but that if Friday could get back to his own nation, he would not only forget all his religion, but all his obligation to me, and would be forward enough to give his countrymen an account of me, and come back perhaps with a hundred or two of them, and make a feast upon me, at which he might be as merry as he used to be with those of his enemies, when they were taken in war. But I wronged the poor honest creature, for which I was very sorry afterwards. However, as my jealousy increased, and held me some weeks, I was a little more circumspect, and not so familiar and kind to him as before. I was every day pumping him, to see if he would discover any of the new thoughts which I suspected were in him; but everything he said was so honest and so innocent that I could find nothing to nourish my suspicion; and, in spite of all my uneasiness, he made me at last entirely his own again; nor did he in the least perceive that I was uneasy, and therefore I could not suspect him of deceit.

One day I said to him, "Friday, do not you wish yourself in your own country, your own nation?" "Yes," he said, "I be much O glad to be at my own nation." "What would you do there?" said I. "Would you turn wild again, eat men's flesh again, and be a savage, as you were before?" He looked full of concern and, shaking his head, said, "No, no; Friday tell them to live good, tell them to pray God, tell them to eat bread, cattle flesh, milk; no eat man again." "Why, then," said I to him, "they will kill you." He looked grave at that, and then said, "No, no, they no kill me, they willing love learn." He meant by this, they would be willing to learn. He added, they learned much of the bearded mans that came in the boat. Then I asked him if he would go back to them. He smiled at that, and told me that he could not swim so far. I told him I would make a canoe for him. He told me he would go if I would go with him. "I go?" says I. "Why, they will eat me, if I come there." "No, no," says he. "Me make they no eat you; me make they much love you." He meant he would tell them how I had killed his enemies and saved his life, and so he would make them love me. Then he told me, as well as he could, how kind they were to the seventeen white men, or bearded men, as he called them, who came on shore there in distress.

AFTER some days, I told Friday I would give him a boat to go back to his own nation; and accordingly I carried him to my canoe, which lay on the other side of the island, and having cleared it of water (for I always kept it sunk in water) I brought it out, showed it to him, and we both went into it. I found he was a most dexterous fellow at managing it, and would make it go almost as swift again as I could. I said to him, "Well, now, Friday, shall you go to your nation?" He looked very dull at my saying so, which, it seems, was because he thought the boat too small to go so far; I then told him I had a bigger; so the next day I went to the place where the first boat lay which I had made, but which I could not get into the water. As I had taken no care of it, and it had lain two or three and twenty years there, the sun had split and dried it, that it was in a manner rotten. But Friday said that such a boat was big enough, and would carry "much enough vittle, drink, bread"; that was his way of talking.

I told him we would go and make one as big as that, and he should go home in it. He answered not one word, but looked very grave and sad. I asked him what was the matter with him. He asked me thus, "Why you angry mad with Friday? What me done?" I told him I was not angry with him at all. "No angry?" says he, repeating the words several times. "Why send Friday home away to my nation?"

"Why," says I, "Friday, did not you say you wished you were there?" "Yes, yes," says he, "wish be both there; no wish Friday there, no master there." "I go there, Friday!" says I. "What shall I do there?" He returned very quick upon me at this: "You do great deal much good," says he. "You teach wild mans be good, sober, tame mans; you tell them know God, pray God, and live new life." "Alas! Friday," says I, "thou knowest not what thou sayest; I am but an ignorant man myself." "Yes, yes," says he, "you teachee me good, you teachee them good." "No, no, Friday," says I, "you shall go without me; leave me here to live by myself, as I did before." He looked confused again at these words; and running to one of the hatchets which he used to wear, he takes it up hastily and gives it to me. "What must I do with this?" says I to him. "You take kill Friday," says he. "What must I kill you for?" said I again. He returns very quick, "What you send Friday away for? Take kill Friday, no send Friday away." This he spoke so earnestly that I saw tears stand in his eyes; in a word, I so plainly discovered the utmost affection in him to me, and a firm resolution in him, that I told him then, and often after, that I would never send him away from me.

Upon the whole, as I found by all his discourse that nothing should part him from me, so I found all the foundation of his desire to go to his own country was laid in his ardent affection to the people, and his hopes of my doing them good; a thing which I had no notion of myself, so I had not the least intention of undertaking it. But I found a strong inclination to attempt an escape, founded on the supposition gathered from the discourse, viz., that there were seventeen bearded men there who might join with me in such an endeavor; and therefore, without any more delay, I went to work with Friday to find out a great tree proper to fell, and make a large canoe to undertake the voyage. There were trees enough in the island to have built a little fleet of good large vessels; but the main thing I looked at was to get one so near the water that we might launch it when it was made, to avoid the mistake I committed at first. At last, Friday pitched upon a tree; for I found he knew much better than I what kind of wood was fittest for it. He was for burning the hollow of this tree out, but I showed him how to cut it with tools, which he did very handily, and in about a month's hard labor we finished it and made it very handsome; especially when, with our axes, we hewed the outside into the true shape of a boat. After this, however, it cost us near a fortnight's time to get her along, as it were inch by inch, upon great rollers into the water; but when she was in, she would have carried twenty men with great ease.

Though she was so big, it amazed me to see with what dexterity, and how swift, my man Friday would manage her, turn her, and paddle her along. So I asked him if we might venture over in her. "Yes," he said, "we venture over in her very well, though great blow wind." However, I had a further design, and that was to make a mast and a sail, and to fit her with an anchor and cable. As to a mast, I pitched upon a straight young cedar tree, which I found near the place; and I set Friday to work to cut it down and gave him directions how to shape and order it. But as to the sail, that was my particular care. I knew I had pieces of old sails enough; but as I had had them now six and twenty years by me, and had not been very careful to preserve them, not imagining that I should ever have this kind of use for them, most of them were rotten. However, I found two pieces which appeared pretty good, and with these I went to work; and with a great deal of pains, and awkward stitching, I at length made a three-cornered ugly thing, like what we call in England a shoulder-of-mutton sail, to go with a boom at bottom, and a little short sprit at the top, such as usually our ships' longboats sail with, and such as I best knew how to manage, as it was such a one I had to the boat in which I had made my escape from Barbary. I was near two months performing this work: making a small stay and a sail, or foresail, to it, to assist if we should turn to windward; and I fixed a rudder to the stern of the canoe to steer with.

After all this was done, I had to teach my man Friday about the navigation of my boat; for, though he knew very well how to paddle a canoe, he knew nothing about a sail and a rudder, and was amazed when he saw me work the boat to and again in the sea by the rudder, and how the sail jibed, and filled this way or that way, as the course we sailed changed. However, with a little use, I made all these things familiar to him, and he became an expert sailor, except that, as to the compass, I could make him understand very little of that. On the other hand, as there was very little cloudy weather, and seldom any fogs in those parts, there was the less occasion for a compass, seeing the stars were always to be seen by night, and the shore by day, except in the rainy seasons, and then nobody cared to stir abroad.

I WAS now entered on the seven and twentieth year of my captivity in this place; though the three last years that I had Friday with me ought rather to be left out of the account, my habitation being quite of another kind than in all the rest of the time. I kept the anniversary of my landing here with the same thankfulness to God for His mercies as at first; and if I had such cause of acknowledgment before, I had much more so now; for I had an invincible impression upon my thoughts that my deliverance was at hand, and that I should not be another year in this place. I went on, however, with my husbandry, digging, planting and fencing, as usual.

The rainy season, in the meantime, came upon us, when we kept more withindoors than at other times. We had stowed our vessel as secure as we could, bringing her up into the creek where I landed my rafts from the ship; and hauling her up to the shore at high-water mark, I made my man Friday dig a little dock, just big enough to hold her, and just deep enough to give her water enough to float in; and then, when the tide was out, we made a strong dam across the end of it to keep the water out; and so she lay dry, as to the tide, from the sea; and, to keep the rain off, we laid a great many boughs of trees, so thick that she was as well thatched as a house; and thus we waited for the months of November and December, in which I designed to make my adventure.

When the fair season began, I called to Friday one morning and bid him go to the seashore and see if he could find a turtle, a thing which we generally got once a week, for the sake of the eggs as well as the flesh. Friday had not been long gone when he came running back, and flew over my outer wall like one that felt not the ground he set his feet on; and before I had time to speak to him, he cried out to me, "O Master! O Master! O sorrow! O bad!" "What's the matter, Friday?" says I. "O yonder, there," says he, "one, two, three canoe: one, two, three!"

The poor fellow trembled and was most terribly scared that they were come to look for him, and would cut him in pieces, and eat him; I comforted him as well as I could, and told him I was in as much danger as he, and that they would eat me as well as him. "But," says I, "Friday, we must resolve to fight them. Can you fight, Friday?" "Me shoot," says he, "but there come many great number." "No matter for that," said I again, "our guns will fright them that we do not kill." So I asked him whether, if I resolved to defend him, he would defend me, and stand by me, and do just as I bid him. He said, "Me die, when you bid die, Master." So I went and fetched a good dram of rum and gave him, for

I had been so good a husband of my rum that I had a great deal left. When he drank it, I made him take the two fowling pieces and loaded them with large swan shot, as big as small pistol bullets; then I took four muskets and loaded them with two slugs and five small bullets each; and my two pistols I loaded with a brace of bullets each. I hung my great sword, as usual, naked by my side, and gave Friday his hatchet. When I had thus prepared, I took my perspective glass, and went up to the side of the hill, to see what I could discover; and I found quickly, by my glass, that there were one and twenty savages, three prisoners, and three canoes; and that their whole business seemed to be the triumphant banquet upon these three human bodies. I observed also that they were landed, not where they had done when Friday made his escape, but nearer to my creek, where the shore was low, and where a thick wood came almost close down to the sea. This, with the abhorrence of the inhuman errand these wretches came about, resolved me to go down to them and kill them all; so I came down again to Friday and asked him if he would stand by me. He had now got over his fright, and told me, as before, he would die when I bid die.

I gave Friday one pistol to stick in his girdle, and three guns upon his shoulder; and I took one pistol and the other three guns myself; and in this posture we marched out. I charged Friday to keep close behind me, and not to do anything till I bid him, and not to speak a word. I went to my right near a mile, as well to get over the creek as to get into the wood, so that I might come within shot of them before I should be discovered.

While I was making this march, however, it returned to my thoughts what occasion, much less what necessity I was in, to attack people who had neither done nor intended me any wrong; who, as to me, were innocent, and whose barbarous customs were their own disaster, that God would punish them whenever He thought fit. It was true that Friday was a declared enemy, and in a state of war with those very particular people, and it was lawful for him to attack them; but I could not say the same with respect to myself. These things were so warmly pressed upon my thoughts that I resolved I would only go and place myself near them, that I might observe their barbarous feast, and that I would act then as God should direct; but that, unless something offered that was more a call to me than yet I knew of, I would not meddle with them.

With this resolution I entered the wood, and with all possible wariness and silence, Friday following close at my heels, I marched till I came to the skirt of the wood, on the side which was next to them. Here I called softly to Friday, and showing him a great tree, which was just at the corner of the wood, I bade him go to the tree and bring me word if he could see there what they were doing. He did so, and came immediately back to me, and told me they might be plainly viewed there; that they were all about their fire, eating the flesh of one of their prisoners, and that another lay bound upon the sand, a little from them, which, he said, they would kill next. He told me it was not one of their nation, but one of the bearded men who had come to their country in the boat. I was filled with horror, and going to the tree, I saw plainly, by my glass, a white man who lay upon the beach of the sea, with his hands and his feet tied with rushes, and that he was a European and had clothes on.

There was another tree, and a little thicket beyond it, about fifty yards nearer to them than the place where I was, which, by going a little way about, I saw I might come at undiscovered, and that then I should be within half a shot of them; so I withheld my passion, though I was indeed enraged to the highest degree; and going back about twenty paces, I got behind some bushes, which held all the way till I came to the other tree; and then came to a little rising ground, which gave me a full view of them, at the distance of about eighty yards.

❧ CHAPTER 18 ❧

I HAD now not a moment to lose, for nineteen of the dreadful wretches sat upon the ground, all close-huddled together, and had just sent the other two to butcher the poor Christian and bring him, perhaps limb by limb, to their fire; and they were stooping down to untie the bands at his feet; I turned to Friday. "Now, Friday," said I, "do exactly as you see me do." So I set down one of the muskets and the fowling piece upon the ground, and Friday did the like by his; and with the other musket I took aim at the savages, bidding him to do the like; then, asking him if he was ready, he said, "Yes." "Then fire at them," said I; and the same moment I fired also.

Friday took his aim so much better than I that on the side that he shot, he killed two of them and wounded three more; and on my side, I killed one and wounded two. They were, you may be sure, in a dreadful consternation;

and all of them who were not hurt jumped upon their feet, but did not immediately know which way to run, or which way to look, for they knew not from whence their destruction came. As soon as the first shot was made, I threw down the piece, and took up the fowling piece, and Friday did the like; he saw me cock and present; he did the same again. "Are you ready, Friday?" said I. "Yes," says he. "Let fly, then," says I, "in the name of God!" And with that, I fired again among the amazed wretches, and so did Friday; and as our pieces were now loaded with what I called swan shot, or small pistol bullets, we found only two dropped, but so many were wounded that they ran about yelling and screaming like mad creatures, all bloody, and most of them miserably wounded, whereof three more fell quickly after, though not quite dead.

"Now, Friday," says I, laying down the discharged pieces, and taking up the musket which was yet loaded, "follow me"; upon which I rushed out of the wood, and showed myself, and Friday close at my foot. As soon as I perceived they saw me, I shouted as loud as I could, and bade Friday do so too; and running as fast as I could, which, by the way, was not very fast, being loaded with arms as I was, I made directly towards the poor victim, who was lying upon the beach between the place where they sat and the sea. The two butchers, who were just going to work with him, had left him at the surprise of our first fire, and fled in a terrible fright to the seaside, and had jumped into a canoe, and three more of the rest made the same way. I turned to Friday and bade him step forwards and fire at them; he understood me immediately, and running about forty yards to be nearer them, he shot at them, and killed two of them and wounded a third.

While my man Friday fired, I pulled out my knife, and cut the rushes that bound the poor victim; and loosing his hands and feet, I lifted him up, and asked him in the Portuguese tongue, what he was. He answered in Latin, "Christianus"; but was so weak and faint that he could scarce stand or speak. I took my bottle out of my pocket and gave it him, making signs that he should drink, which he did; and I gave him a piece of bread, which he ate. Then I asked him what countryman he was, and he said, "Espagñol"; and being a little recovered, let me know by all the signs he could make how much he was in my debt for his deliverance. "Señor," said I, with as much Spanish as I could make up, "we will talk afterwards, but we must fight now; if you have any strength left, take this pistol and sword, and lay about you." He took them very thankfully; and no sooner had he the arms in his hands but, as if they had put new vigor into him, he flew upon his murderers like a fury, and had cut two of them in pieces in an instant; for the truth is, as the whole was a surprise to them, so the poor creatures were so much frightened with the noise of our pieces that they fell down for mere amazement and fear, and had no more power to attempt their own escape than their flesh had to resist our shot; and that was the case of those five that Friday shot at in the boat; for as three of them fell with the hurt they received, so the other two fell with the fright.

I kept my piece in my hand, still without firing, being willing to keep my charge ready, because I had given the Spaniard my pistol and sword; so I called to Friday, and bade him run up to the tree from whence we first fired, and fetch the arms which lay there that had been discharged, which he did with great swiftness; and then giving him my musket, I sat down myself to load all the rest again, and bade them come to me when they wanted. While I was loading these pieces, there happened a fierce engagement between the Spaniard and one of the savages, who made at him with one of their great wooden swords, the same like weapon that was to have killed him before if I had not prevented it. The Spaniard, who was as bold and brave as could be imagined, though weak, had fought this Indian a good while, and had cut him two great wounds on his head; but the savage, being a stout, lusty fellow, closing in with him, had thrown him down, and was wringing my sword out of his hand; when the Spaniard, though undermost, wisely quitted the sword, drew the pistol from his girdle, shot the savage through the body, and killed him upon the spot, before I, who was running to help him, could come near him.

Friday, being now left to his liberty, pursued the flying wretches with no weapon in his hand but his hatchet; and with that he dispatched all he could come up with; and, the Spaniard coming to me for a gun, I gave him one of the fowling pieces, with which he pursued two of the savages, and wounded them both; but as he was not able to run, they both got from him into the wood, where Friday pursued them, and killed one, but the other was too nimble for him; and though he was wounded, yet plunged himself into the sea, and swam, with all his might, off to those who were left in the canoe, so that of all the savages only four had escaped our hands.

Those that were in the canoe worked hard to get out of gunshot, and Friday would fain have had me take one of their canoes and pursue them. Indeed, I was very anxious about their escape, lest, carrying the news home to their people, they should come back perhaps with two or three hundred canoes, and devour us by mere multitude; so I consented to pursue them, and running to one of their canoes, I jumped in and bade Friday follow me; but when I was in the canoe, I was surprised to find another poor creature lying there, bound hand and foot. He had been tied so long that he had really but little life in him. I immediately cut the twisted rushes, which they had bound him with, and would have helped him up; but he could not stand or speak, but groaned most piteously, believing that he was only unbound in order to be killed. When Friday came to him, I bade him speak to him and tell him of his deliverance and, pulling out my bottle, made him give the poor wretch a dram, which, with the news of his being delivered, revived him, and he sat up in the boat. But when Friday came to hear him speak, and look in his face, it would have moved anyone into tears to have seen how Friday kissed him, embraced him, hugged him, cried, laughed, hallooed, jumped about, danced, sung; then cried again, wrung his hands, beat his own face and head, and then sung and jumped about again, like a distracted creature. It was a good while before I could make him tell me what was the matter; but when he came a little to himself, he told me that it was his father.

It is not easy for me to express how it moved me to see what ecstasy and filial affection had worked in this poor savage at the sight of his father, and of his being delivered from death, nor, indeed, can I describe half the extravagancies of his affection after this; for he went into the boat and out of the boat a great many times; when he went in to him, he would sit down by him, open his breast, and hold his father's head close to his bosom for many minutes together, to comfort it; then he took his arms and ankles, which were numbed and stiff with the binding, and chafed and rubbed them with his hands; and I gave him some rum out of my bottle to rub them with, which did them a great deal of good.

This affair put an end to our pursuit of the canoe with the other savages, who were got now almost out of sight; and it blew so hard within two hours after, and before they could be got a quarter of their way, and continued blowing so hard all night, and that from the northwest, which was against them, that I could not suppose they ever reached their own coast.

But to return to Friday: he was so busy about his father that I could not find in my heart to take him off for some time; but after I thought he could leave him a little, I called him to me, and he came jumping and laughing, and pleased to the highest extreme. Then I gave him some bread out of a little pouch I carried, also a dram for himself, but he would not taste it, but carried it to his father. I had in my pocket two bunches of raisins, so I gave him a handful. He had no sooner given his father these raisins but I saw him come out of the boat, and run away as if he had been bewitched. He was the swiftest fellow on his feet that ever I saw; he was out of sight in an instant, though I called and hallooed after him; and in a quarter of an hour he came back, though not so fast as he went; and as he came nearer, I found his pace was slacker, because he had something in his hand. When he came up to me, I found he had been quite home for an earthen jug to bring his father some fresh water, and that he had two more loaves of bread. The water revived his father more than all the rum I had given him, for he was fainting with thirst.

When his father had drunk, I bade Friday give some to the poor Spaniard, who was in as much want of it as his father; and I sent one of the loaves that Friday brought to the Spaniard, too, who was indeed very weak, and was reposing himself upon a green place under the shade of a tree; and whose limbs were stiff, and swelled with the rude bandage he had been tied with. When I saw that upon Friday's coming to him with the water, he sat up and drank, and took the bread, and began to eat, I went to him and gave him a handful of raisins; he looked up in my face with all the tokens of gratitude that could appear in any countenance, but was so weak that he could not stand up upon his feet; so I bade him sit still and caused Friday to rub his ankles, and bathe them with rum, as he had done his father's.

I then told the Spaniard to let Friday help him up, if he could, and lead him to the boat, and then we would take him to our dwelling. But Friday, a lusty strong fellow, took the Spaniard quite up upon his back, and carried him away to the boat, and set him down close to his father; and then launched the boat, and paddled it along the shore faster than I could walk, though the wind blew pretty hard too; so he brought them both safe into our creek and, leaving them in the boat, ran to fetch the other canoe; and he had it in the creek almost as soon as I got to it by land; so he wafted me over and then went to help our new guests out of the boat, which he did; but they were neither of them able to walk.

To remedy this, I soon made a kind of a handbarrow to lay them on, and Friday and I carried them both up together upon it, between us. But when we got them to the outside of our wall, or fortification, we were at a worse loss than before, for it was impossible to get them over, and I was resolved not to break it down. So I set to work again; and Friday and I, in about two hours' time, made a very handsome tent, covered with old sails, and above that with boughs of trees, being in the space between our outward fence and the grove of young wood which I had planted; and here we made them two beds of good rice straw, with blankets laid upon it to lie on, and another to cover them, on each bed.

⊰⧽| CHAPTER 19 |⧼⊱

MY ISLAND was now peopled, and I thought myself rich in subjects; and it was a merry reflection, which I frequently made, how like a king I looked. First of all, the whole country was my own property, so that I had an undoubted right of dominion. Secondly, I was absolutely lord and lawgiver; my people all owed their lives to me, and were ready to lay down their lives, if there had been occasion for it, for me. It was remarkable, too, I had but three subjects, and they were of three different religions: my man Friday was a Protestant, his father was a Pagan, and the Spaniard was a Papist; however, I allowed liberty of conscience throughout my dominions. But this is by the way.

As soon as I had given the two rescued men shelter, I ordered Friday to kill a yearling goat of my flock. I cut off the hinder quarter, and chopping it into small pieces, I set Friday to work to boiling and stewing, and made them a very good dish of flesh and broth, having put some barley and rice also into the broth. And, having set a table in the new tent for them, I sat down, and ate my dinner also with them, and, as well as I could, cheered them, and encouraged them. Friday was my interpreter, especially to his father, and, indeed, to the Spaniard too; for the Spaniard spoke the language of the savages pretty well.

Then I ordered Friday to take one of the canoes, and go and fetch our muskets and other firearms, which, for want of time, we had left upon the place of battle; and, the next day, I ordered him to go and bury the dead bodies of the savages, which lay open to the sun, and would presently be offensive. I also ordered him to bury the horrid remains of their barbarous feast, which I could not think of doing myself; all which he punctually performed, and effaced the very appearance of the savages being there; so that when I went again, I could scarce know where it was, otherwise than by the corner of the wood pointing to the place.

I then began to enter into a little conversation with my two subjects; and, first, I set Friday to inquire of his father what he thought of the escape of the savages in that canoe, and whether we might expect a return of them, with a power too great for us to resist. His first opinion was that the savages in the boat could never live out the storm which blew that night they went off, but must be drowned, or driven south to other shores, where they were sure to be devoured; but, as to what they would do if they came safe home, he said it was his opinion that they were so frightened with the manner of their being attacked, the noise, and the fire, that he believed they would tell the people that the others were all killed by thunder and lightning, not by the hand of man; and that Friday and I were two heavenly spirits, or furies, come down to destroy them, and not men with weapons. And this old savage was right, for, as I have learned since, the savages never attempted to go over to the island afterwards, they were so terrified with the accounts given by those four men (for, it seems, they did escape the sea) that they believed whoever went to that enchanted island would be destroyed by fire from the gods. This, however, I knew not for a good while; and therefore was kept always upon my guard, with all my army; for, as there were now four of us, I would have ventured upon a hundred of them, fairly in the open field, at any time.

In a little time, however, no more canoes appearing, the fear of their coming wore off; and I began to take my former thoughts of a voyage to the main into consideration; being assured, by Friday's father, that I might depend upon good usage from their nation on his account, if I would go. But my thoughts were a little suspended when I had a serious discourse with the Spaniard, and when I understood that there were sixteen more of his countrymen and Portuguese, who, having been cast away there, lived at peace with the savages, but were sore put to it for necessaries. He told me they had some arms with them, but they were perfectly useless, for that they had neither powder nor ball, the washing of the sea having spoiled all their powder but a little, which they used at their first landing, to provide themselves some food.

I asked what he thought would become of them there, and if they had formed no design of making any escape. He said they had many consultations about it; but that having neither vessel, nor tools to build one, nor provisions of any kind, their councils always ended in tears and despair. I asked him how he thought they would receive a proposal from me, which might tend towards an escape; and I told him, with freedom, I feared mostly their treachery and ill usage of me if I put my life in their hands, for that gratitude was no inherent virtue in the nature of man, nor did men always square their dealings by the obligations they had received, so much as they did by the advantages they expected. I told him it would be very hard that I should be the instrument of their deliverance, and that they should afterwards make me their prisoner in New Spain, where an Englishman, what accident soever brought him thither, was certain to be delivered up to the Inquisition. I added that otherwise I was persuaded we might, with so many hands, build a bark large enough to carry us all away, either to the Brazils, southward, or to the islands, or the Spanish coast, northward; but that if they should, when I had put weapons into their hands, carry me by force among their own people, I might make my case worse than it was before.

He answered, with a great deal of candor and ingenuousness, that their condition was so miserable, and they were so sensible of it, that he believed they would abhor the thought of using any man unkindly that should contribute to their deliverance; and that if I pleased, he would go to them with the old man, and discourse with them about it, and return again, and bring me their answer; that he would make conditions with them, upon their solemn oath, that they should be absolutely under my leading, as their commander and captain; and that they should swear, upon the holy sacraments and gospel, to be true to me, and go to such Christian country as that I should agree to, and no other, and to be directed wholly by my orders, till they were landed safely in such country as I intended; and that he would bring a contract from them, under their hands, for that purpose. Then he told me he would first swear to me himself that he would never stir from me as long as he lived, till I gave him orders; and that he would take my side to the last drop of his blood, if there should happen the least breach of faith among his countrymen. He told me they were all very civil, honest men; and that he was sure, if I would undertake their relief, they would live and die by me.

Upon these assurances, I resolved to send the old savage and this Spaniard over to them to treat. But when we had got all things in readiness to go, the Spaniard himself started an objection, which had so much prudence in it, on one hand, and so much sincerity, on the other hand, that I put off the deliverance of his comrades for at least half a year. The case was thus: he had been with us now about a month, during which time I had let him see in what manner I had provided, with the assistance of Providence, for my support, and he saw what stock of barley and rice I had laid up; which, though it was more than sufficient for myself, yet it was not sufficient, without good husbandry, for my family, now it was increased to four; but much less would it be sufficient if his countrymen, who were, as he said, sixteen, still alive, should come over; and least of all would it be sufficient to victual our vessel, if we should build one, for a voyage to any of the Christian colonies of America; so he told me he thought we should dig and cultivate some more land, as much as I could spare seed to sow, and that we should wait another harvest, that we might have a supply of grain for his countrymen, when they should come; for want might be a temptation to them to disagree, or not to think themselves delivered otherwise than out of one difficulty into another. "You know," says he, "the children of Israel, though they rejoiced at first for their being delivered out of Egypt, yet they rebelled even against God himself, that delivered them, when they came to want bread in the Wilderness."

His caution was so seasonable, and his advice so good, that I could not but be very well pleased with his proposal, as well as I was satisfied with his fidelity; so we fell to digging, all four of us, as well as the wooden tools we were furnished with permitted; and in about a month's time, by the end of which it was seedtime, we had got enough land prepared to sow two and twenty bushels of barley and sixteen jars of rice, which was all the seed we had to spare; nor, indeed, did we leave ourselves barely sufficient for our own food for the six months that we had to expect our crop.

Our number being now sufficient to put us out of fear of the savages, if they had come, unless their number had been very great, we went freely all over the island, whenever we found occasion; and as we had our escape upon our thoughts, it was impossible, at least for me, to have the means of it out of mine. For this purpose, I marked out several trees which I thought fit for our work, and I set Friday and his father to cutting them down; and I caused the Spaniard to oversee and direct them. I showed them with what indefatigable pains I had hewed a large tree into single planks, and I caused them to do the like, till they had made about a dozen large planks of good oak, near two feet broad, thirty-five feet long, and from two inches to four inches thick; what prodigious labor it took up, anyone may imagine.

At the same time, I contrived to increase my little flock of tame goats; I made Friday and the Spaniard go out one day, and myself with Friday the next day, and by this means we got about twenty young kids; for whenever we shot the dam, we saved the kids. But, above all, the season for curing the grapes coming on, I caused such a prodigious quantity to be hung up in the sun that I believe we could have filled sixty or eighty barrels; and these, with our bread, were a great part of our food—and very good living, too, for they are exceedingly nourishing.

It was now harvest, and our crop was not the most plentiful increase I had seen in the island, but it was enough to answer our end; for from twenty-two bushels of barley we brought in and threshed out above two hundred and twenty bushels, and the like in proportion of rice; which was store enough for our food to the next harvest, though all the sixteen Spaniards had been on shore with me; or it would plentifully have victualed our ship to have carried us to any part of America. When we had housed and secured our magazine of grain, we fell to work to make more baskets in which to keep it; and the Spaniard was very handy and dexterous at this part.

And now I gave the Spaniard leave to go over to the mainland. I gave him a strict charge not to bring any man with him who would not first swear, in the presence of himself and the old savage, that he would no way injure, fight with, or attack the person he should find in the island, who was so kind as to deliver them; but that they would stand by him, and defend him against all such attempts, and wherever they went would be entirely subjected to his command; and that this should be put in writing and signed with their hands. How they were to have done this, when I knew they had neither pen nor ink, was a question which we never asked. Under these instructions, the Spaniard and the old savage, the father of Friday, went away in one of the canoes which they were brought in when they came as prisoners to be devoured by the savages. I gave each of them a musket, with a firelock on it, and about eight charges of powder and ball, charging them to be very good husbands of both, and not to use either of them but upon urgent occasions.

This was a cheerful work, being the first measures used by me, in view of my deliverance, for now twenty-seven years and some days. I gave them bread and dried grapes, sufficient for themselves for many days, and sufficient for all the Spaniards for about eight days' time; and wishing them a good voyage, I saw them go; agreeing with them about a signal they should hang out at their return, by which I should know them when they came back, before they came on shore. They went away on the day that the moon was at full, by my account in the month of October.

IT WAS no less than eight days I had waited for them, when a strange and unforeseen accident intervened, of which the like has not perhaps been heard of in history. I was fast asleep in my hutch one morning, when my man Friday came running in to me, and called aloud, "Master, Master, they are come, they are come!" I jumped up, and, regardless of danger, I went out as soon as I could get my clothes on, through my little grove, which, by the way, was by this time grown to be a very thick wood; I say, regardless of danger, I went without my arms, which it was not my custom to do; but I was surprised when, turning my eyes to the sea, I presently saw a boat about a league and a half distance, standing in for the shore, with a shoulder-of-mutton sail, and the wind blowing pretty fair to bring them in; also I observed that they did not come from that side which the shore lay on, but from the southernmost end of the island. Upon this, I called Friday in, and bade him lie close, for these were not the people we looked for, and we could not know yet whether they were friends or enemies.

In the next place, I went in to fetch my perspective glass, to see what I could make of them; and having taken the ladder out, I climbed up to the top of the hill, to take my view the plainer without being discovered. I had scarce set my foot upon the hill, when my eye plainly discovered a ship lying at an anchor, at about two leagues and a half distance from me, south-southeast, but not above a league and a half from the shore. By my observation, it appeared plainly to be an English ship, and the boat appeared to be an English longboat.

I cannot express the confusion I was in, though the joy of seeing a ship, and one that I had reason to believe was manned by my own countrymen, was such as I cannot describe; but yet I had some secret doubts about me, bidding me to keep upon my guard. In the first place, it occurred to me to consider what business an English ship could have here, since it was not the way to or from any part of the world where the English had any traffic; and I knew there had been no storms to drive them in there, as in distress; and that if they were really English, it was most probable that they were here upon no good design; and that I had better continue as I was than fall into the hands of thieves and murderers.

Let no man despise the secret hints and notices of danger, which sometimes are given him when he may think there is no possibility of its being real; for had I not been made cautious by this secret admonition, I had been undone inevitably, and in a far worse condition than before.

I presently saw the boat draw near the shore, and then run upon the beach at about half a mile from me. When they were on shore, I was fully satisfied they were Englishmen, at least most of them; there were in all eleven men, whereof three were unarmed; and when the first four or five of them were jumped on shore, they took those three out of the boat as prisoners; one of the three I could perceive using the most passionate gestures of entreaty and despair, even to a kind of extravagance; the other two lifted up their hands sometimes, and appeared concerned, but not to such a degree as the first. I was confounded at the sight, and knew not what the meaning of it should be. Friday called out to me in English, as well as he could, "O Master! You see English mans eat prisoner as well as savage mans." "Why, Friday," says I, "do you think they are going to eat them?" "Yes," says Friday, "they will eat them." "No, no," says I. "Friday, I am afraid they will murder them, indeed, but you may be sure they will not eat them."

All this while I had no thought of what the matter really was, but stood trembling with the horror of the sight, expecting every moment when the three prisoners should be killed; nay, once I saw one of the villains lift up his arm with a great cutlass to strike one of the poor men; and I expected to see him fall every moment, at which all the blood in my body seemed to run chill in my veins. I wished heartily now for my Spaniard, and the savage that was gone with him, or that I had any way to have come undiscovered within shot of them, that I might have rescued the three men; but it fell out another way. After I had observed the outrageous usage of the three men by the insolent seamen, I observed the fellows run scattering about the island, as if they wanted to see the country. I observed that the three other men had liberty to go also where they pleased; but they sat down all three upon the ground, very pensive, and looked like men in despair.

This put me in mind of the first time when I came on shore and began to look about me: how I gave myself over for lost; how wildly I looked around me; what dreadful apprehensions I had; and how I lodged in the tree all night, for fear of being devoured by wild beasts. As I knew nothing that night of the supply I was to receive by the providential driving of the ship nearer the land by the

storms and tide, by which I have since been so long nour-
ished and supported, so these three poor desolate men
knew nothing how certain of deliverance and supply they
were, how near it was to them, and how really they were
in a condition of safety, at the same time that they
thought themselves lost, and their case desperate.

⊰⧉ CHAPTER 20 ⧉⊱

IT WAS just at the top of high water when these people came on shore; and they carelessly stayed till the tide was spent and the water was ebbed considerably away, leaving their boat aground. They left two men in the boat, who, as I found afterwards, having drunk a little too much brandy, fell asleep; however, one of them waking a little sooner than the other, and finding the boat too fast aground for him to stir it, hallooed out for the rest, who were straggling about; upon which they all soon came to the boat; but it was past all their strength to launch her, the boat being very heavy, and the shore on that side being a soft oozy sand, almost like a quicksand. In this condition, like true seamen, who are perhaps the least of all mankind given to forethought, they gave it over, and away they strolled about the country again; and I heard one of them say aloud to another, calling them off from the boat, "Why, let her alone, Jack, can't you? She'll float next tide"; by which I was fully confirmed of what countrymen they were. All this while I kept myself very close, not once daring to stir out of my castle any farther than to my place of observation, near the top of the hill; and very glad I was to think how well it was fortified. I knew it was no less than ten hours before the boat could float again, and by that time it would be dark, and I might be at more liberty to see their motions, and to hear their discourse. In the meantime, I fitted myself up for a battle, as before, though with more caution, knowing I had to do with another kind of enemy than I had at first. I took myself two fowling pieces, and I gave Friday three muskets. My figure, indeed, was very fierce; I had my formidable goat's-skin coat on, with my great cap, a naked sword by my side, two pistols in my belt, and a gun upon each shoulder.

It was my design, as I said above, not to have made any attempt till it was dark; but about two o'clock, being the heat of the day, I found that they were all gone straggling into the woods, and as I thought, laid down to sleep. The three poor distressed men, too anxious for their condition to get any sleep, were sat down under the shelter of a great tree, at about a quarter of a mile from me, and as I thought, out of sight of any of the rest. Upon this I resolved to discover myself to them, and learn something of their condition; immediately I marched forth, my man Friday at a good distance behind me, as formidable for his arms as I, but not making quite so staring a specterlike figure as I did. I came as near them undiscovered as I could, and then, before any of them saw me, I called aloud to them in Spanish, "What are ye, gentlemen?" They started up at the noise, but were ten times more confounded when they saw me and the uncouth figure that I made. They made no answer at all, but I thought I perceived them just going to fly from me, when I spoke to them in English: "Gentlemen," said I, "do not be surprised at me; perhaps you may have a friend near, when you did not expect it." "He must be sent directly from Heaven then," said one of them very gravely to me, and pulling off his hat at the same time to me, "for our condition is past the help of man." "All help is from Heaven, sir," said I. "But can you put a stranger in the way how to help you? You seem to be in some great distress. I saw you when you landed; and when you seemed to make supplication to the brutes that came with you, I saw one of them lift up his sword as if to kill you."

The poor man, with tears running down his face, and trembling, looking like one astonished, returned, "Am I talking to God or man? Is it a real man or an angel?" "Be in no fear about that, sir," said I. "If God had sent an angel to relieve you, he would have come better clothed, and armed after another manner than you see me; pray lay aside your fears; I am a man, an Englishman, and disposed to assist you; you see I have one servant only; we have arms and ammunition; tell us freely, what is your case?"

"Our case," said he, "is too long to tell you, while our

murderers are so near us; but, in short, sir, I was commander of that ship, my men have mutinied against me; they have been hardly prevailed on not to murder me and at last have set me on shore in this desolate place, with these two men with me, one my mate, the other a passenger, where we expected to perish, believing the place to be uninhabited."

"Where are these brutes?" said I. "There they lie, sir," said he, pointing to a thicket of trees. "My heart trembles for fear they have seen us, and heard you speak; if they have, they will certainly murder us all." "Have they any firearms?" said I. He answered they had only two pieces, one of which they left in the boat. "Well, then," said I, "leave the rest to me; I see they are all asleep, it is an easy thing to kill them all; but shall we rather take them prisoners?" He told me there were two desperate villains among them that it was scarce safe to show any mercy to; but if they were secured, he believed the rest would return to their duty. I asked him which they were. He told me he could not at that distance distinguish them, but he would obey my orders in anything I would direct. "Well," says I, "let us retreat out of their view or hearing, lest they awake, and we will resolve further." So they willingly went back with me, till the woods covered us from their enemies.

"Look you, sir," said I, "if I venture upon your deliverance, are you willing to make two conditions with me?" He anticipated my proposals, by telling me that both he and the ship, if recovered, should be wholly directed and commanded by me in everything; and, if the ship was not recovered, he would live and die with me in what part of the world soever I would send him, and the two other men said the same. "Well," says I, "my conditions are but two: first, that while you stay in this island with me, you will not pretend to any authority here; and if I put arms in your hands, you will, upon all occasions, give them up to me and do no prejudice to me or mine upon this island and, in the meantime, be governed by my orders; secondly, that if the ship is recovered, you will carry me and my man to England, passage free."

He gave me all the assurances that the invention or faith of man could devise that he would comply with these most reasonable demands; and, besides, would owe his life to me, and acknowledge it upon all occasions, as long as he lived. "Well then," said I, "here are three muskets for you, with powder and ball; tell me next what you think is proper to be done." He showed me all the testimonies of his gratitude that he was able, but offered to be wholly guided by me. I told him the best method I could think of was to fire upon them at once, as they lay, and if any was not killed at the first volley, and offered to submit, we might save them, and so put it wholly upon God's providence to direct the shot. He said that he was loath to kill them, if he could help it; but that those two were incorrigible villains, and had been the authors of all the mutiny in the ship, and if they escaped, we should be undone still; for they would go on board and bring the whole ship's company, and destroy us all. "Well then," says I, "necessity legitimates my advice." However, seeing him still cautious of shedding blood, I told him they should go themselves and manage as they found convenient.

In the middle of this discourse we heard some of them awake, and soon after we saw two of them on their feet. I asked him if either of them were the heads of the mutiny. He said, "No." "Well then," said I, "you may let them escape; and Providence seems to have awakened them on purpose to save themselves. Now," says I, "if the rest escape you, it is your fault."

Animated with this, he took the musket I had given him in his hand, and a pistol in his belt, and his two comrades with him, with each a piece in his hand; the two men who were with him going first made some noise, at which one of the seamen who was awake turned about, and seeing them coming, cried out to the rest; but it was too late then, for the moment he cried out they fired; the captain wisely reserving his own piece. They had so well aimed their shot at the two villains whom they knew, that they were killed on the spot. There were three more in the company, and one of them was also slightly wounded. By this time I was come; and when they saw their danger, and that it was in vain to resist, they begged for mercy. The captain told them he would spare their lives, if they would give him any assurance of their abhorrence of the treachery they had been guilty of, and would swear to be faithful to him in recovering the ship, and afterwards in carrying her back to

Jamaica, from whence they came. They gave him all the protestations of their sincerity that could be desired, and he was willing to believe them, and spare their lives, which I was not against, only that I obliged him to keep them bound hand and foot while they were on the island.

While this was doing, I sent Friday with the captain's mate to the boat, with orders to secure her, and bring away the oars and sails, which they did; and by and by three straggling men, that were (happily for them) parted from the rest, came back upon hearing the guns fired, and seeing the captain, who before was their prisoner, now their conqueror, they submitted to be bound also; and so our victory was complete.

It now remained that I should tell the captain my history, which he heard with an attention even to amazement; and particularly at the wonderful manner of my being furnished with provisions and ammunition; and, indeed, as my story is a whole collection of wonders, it affected him deeply. But when he reflected from thence upon himself, and how I seemed to have been preserved there on purpose to save his life, the tears ran down his face, and he could not speak a word more. After this communication was at an end, I took him and his two men into my apartment, where I refreshed them with such provisions as I had, and showed them all the contrivances I had made during my long, long inhabiting that place.

The captain admired my fortification, and how perfectly I had concealed my retreat with a grove of trees, which, having been now planted near twenty years, and the trees growing much faster than in England, was become a little wood, and so thick that it was impassable in any part of it but at that one side where I had reserved my little winding passage into it. I told him this was my castle and my residence, but that I had a seat in the country, as most princes have, whither I could retreat upon occasion, and I would show him that too another time; but at present our business was to consider how to recover the ship. He agreed with me as to that; but told me he was perfectly at a loss what measures to take, for that there were still six and twenty hands on board, who, having entered into a cursed conspiracy, by which they had all forfeited their lives to the law, would be hardened in it now by desperation, and would carry it on, knowing that, if they were subdued, they would be brought to the gallows as soon as they came to England, or to any of the English colonies; and that, therefore, there would be no attacking them with so small a number as we were.

I mused for some time upon what he had said, and found it was a very rational conclusion, and that, therefore, something was to be resolved on speedily, as well to draw the men on board into some snare for their surprise, as to prevent their landing upon us, and destroying us. It presently occurred to me that in a little while the ship's crew, wondering what was become of their comrades and of the boat, would certainly come on shore in their other boat to look for them; and that then, perhaps, they might come armed and be too strong for us; this he allowed to be rational. Upon this, I told him the first thing we had to do was to stave the boat, which lay upon the beach, so that they might not carry her off; accordingly we went on board, took the arms which were left on board out of her, and whatever else we found there, which was a bottle of brandy, and another of rum, a few biscuit cakes, a horn of powder, and a great lump of sugar in a piece of canvas; all which was very welcome to me, especially the brandy and sugar, of which I had none left for many years.

When we had carried all these things on shore, as well as the oars, mast, sail and rudder, and had heaved the boat upon the beach so high that the tide would not float her off at high-water mark, and besides had broke a hole in her bottom too big to be quickly stopped, and were set down musing what we should do, we heard the ship fire a gun, and saw her make a waft with her ensign as a signal for the boat to come on board. They fired several times, making other signals for the boat. At last, when all their signals and firing proved fruitless, and they found the boat did not stir, we saw them, by the help of my glasses, hoist another boat out, and row towards the shore; and we found, as they approached, that there were no less than ten men in her, and that they had firearms.

⊰ CHAPTER 21 ⊱

WE HAD a full view of them as they came, and a plain sight even of their faces; because they rowed up under shore to come to the same place where the boat lay; and the captain knew the characters of all the men in the boat, of whom, he said, there were three very honest fellows, who, he was sure, were led into this conspiracy by the rest, being overpowered and frightened; but that, as for the boatswain, who, it seems, was the chief officer among them, and all the rest, they were outrageous, and were no doubt made desperate in their new enterprise; and terribly apprehensive he was that they would be too powerful for us.

I smiled at him, and told him that men in our circumstances were past the operation of fear, seeing almost every condition that could be was better than that which we were in. "And where, sir," said I, "is your belief of my being preserved here on purpose to save your life, which elevated you a little while ago? For my part, there seems to me but one thing amiss." "What is that?" says he. "Why," says I, "it is, that as you say there are three or four honest fellows among them, which should be spared; had they been all wicked, I should have thought God's providence had delivered them into your hands; for, depend upon it, every man that comes ashore shall die or live as he behaves to us." As I spoke this with a cheerful countenance, I found it greatly encouraged him; so we set vigorously to our business.

We had, upon the first appearance of the boat's coming from the ship, considered of separating our prisoners. Two of them, of whom the captain was less assured than ordinary, I sent with Friday and one of the three delivered men, to my cave, where they were out of danger of being discovered. Here they left them bound, but gave them provisions; and promised them, if they continued there quietly, to give them their liberty in a day or two; but that, if they attempted their escape, they should be put to death without mercy. They promised to bear their confinement with patience, and were very thankful that they had such good usage as to have provisions and light left them; for Friday gave them candles (such as we made ourselves) for their comfort, and they did not know but that he stood sentinel at the entrance.

Two of the other prisoners were kept pinioned, because the captain was not free to trust them; but the other two were taken into my service, upon the captain's recommendation, and upon their solemnly engaging to live and die with us; so with them and the three honest men we were seven men well armed; and I made no doubt we should be able to deal well enough with the ten that were coming, considering that the captain had said that there were three or four honest men among them also. As soon as they got to the place where their other boat lay, they ran their boat into the beach, and came on shore. They ran then to their other boat; and it was easy to see they were under a great surprise to find her stripped of all that was in her, and a great hole in her bottom. After they had mused a while upon this, they set up two or three great shouts, hallooing with all their might, to try if they could make their companions hear; but all was to no purpose; then they fired a volley of their small arms, and the echoes made the woods ring; but those in our keeping durst give no answer. They were so astonished at this that, as they told us afterwards, they resolved to go on board again to their ship, and let them know that the men were all murdered, and the longboat staved; accordingly, they immediately launched their boat again, and got all of them in it.

The captain was confounded at this, believing they would go on board the ship again, and set sail, giving their comrades over for lost, and so he should still lose the ship, but he was quickly as much frightened the other way.

They had not been long put off with the boat but we perceived them coming on shore again; but this time they left three men in the boat. Now we were at a loss what to do, as our seizing those seven men on shore would be no advantage to us if we let the boat escape, because they would then row away to the ship, and then the rest of them would be sure to weigh and set sail. We had no remedy but to wait and see what might happen. The seven men came on shore, and the three who remained in the boat put her off to a good distance, and came to an anchor where it was impossible for us to come at them. Those that came on shore kept close together, marching towards the top of the little hill under which my habitation lay; and we could see them plainly, though they could not perceive us. When they were come to the brow of the hill, where they could see into the woods, they shouted and hallooed till they were weary; and not caring, it seems, to venture far from the shore, nor far from one another, they sat down together under a tree to consider it. Had they gone to sleep there as the other part of them had done, they had done the job for us; but they were too full of apprehensions of danger to venture to go to sleep, though they could not tell what the danger was they had to fear.

We lay still a long time, very irresolute what course to take. At length, we saw them all start up, and march down towards the sea. I imagined that they had given over their search, and I thought of a stratagem to fetch them back again. I ordered Friday and the captain's mate to go over the creek westward to a little rising ground, at about half a mile distance, and halloo out, as loud as they could. As soon as they heard the seamen answer them, they should halloo in return; and then, keeping out of sight, make a circle into the woods, always answering when the others hallooed, to draw them into the island.

The men were just going into the boat when Friday and the mate hallooed, and answering, the men ran along the shore westward, towards the voices. They were presently stopped by the creek, where, the water being up, they could not get over, and called for the boat to come up and set them over; as, indeed, I expected. When they had set themselves over, the boat being gone a good way into the creek, they took one of the three men out of her, to go along with them, and left only two in the boat, having fastened her to the stump of a little tree on the shore. This was what I wished for; and immediately, leaving Friday and the captain's mate to their business, I took the rest with me, and crossing the creek out of their sight, we surprised the two men before they were aware; one of them lying on the shore, and the other being in the boat. The fellow on shore was between sleeping and waking; and the captain, who was foremost, ran in upon him and knocked him down, and then called out to him in the boat to yield, or he was a dead man. There needed very few arguments to persuade a single man to yield, when he saw five men upon him and his comrade knocked down;

besides, this was, it seems, one of the three who were not so hearty in the mutiny as the rest of the crew. In the meantime, Friday and the captain's mate so well managed their business with the rest that they drew them, by hallooing and answering, from one hill to another, and from one wood to another, till they not only heartily tired them, but left them where they were sure they could not reach back to the boat before dark; and, indeed, they were heartily tired themselves, by the time they came back to us.

We had nothing now to do but to watch for them in the dark, and to fall upon them. It was several hours after Friday came back to me before they came back to their boat; and we could hear the foremost of them, long before they came quite up, calling to those behind to come along; and could hear them answer, and complain how lame and tired they were, and not able to come any faster, which was welcome news to us. At length they came up to the boat; but it is impossible to express their confusion when they found the boat fast aground in the creek, the tide ebbed out, and their two men gone. We could hear them call to one another in a most lamentable manner, telling one another they were got into an enchanted island with devils and spirits in it, and they should be all carried away and devoured. They hallooed again and called their two comrades by their names many times; but no answer. After some time, we could see them, by the little light there was, run about, wringing their hands like men in despair; and that sometimes they would go and sit down in the boat to rest themselves, then come ashore again and walk about again. My men would fain have had me give them leave to fall upon them at once in the dark; but I wished to kill as few of them as I could; and especially I was unwilling to hazard the killing any of our men, knowing the others were well armed. I resolved to wait, to see if they did not separate; and to make sure of them, I drew my ambuscade nearer and ordered Friday and the captain to creep upon their hands and knees and get as near them as they could before they offered to fire.

They had not been long in that posture, when the boatswain, who was the principal ringleader of the mutiny, came walking towards them with two more of the crew; the captain was so eager at having this principal rogue in his power that he hardly had the patience to let him come so near as to be sure of him. But when they came nearer, the captain and Friday, starting up on their feet, let fly at them. The boatswain was killed upon the spot; the next man was shot in the body, and fell just by him, though he did not die till an hour after; and the third ran for it. At the noise of the fire, I immediately advanced with my whole army, which was now eight men, viz., myself, generalissimo; Friday, my lieutenant general; the captain and his two men; and the three prisoners of war whom we had trusted with arms. We came upon the mutineers in the dark, so that they could not see our number; and I made the man they had left in the boat, who was now one of us, call to them by name, to try if I could bring them to a parley.

He called out, as loud as he could, to one of them, "Tom Smith! Tom Smith!" Tom Smith answered immediately, "Is that Robinson?" For he knew the voice. The other answered, "Aye, aye. For God's sake, Tom Smith, throw down your arms and yield, or you are all dead men this moment." "Who must we yield to? Where are they?" says Smith. "Here they are," says he. "Here's our captain and fifty men with him, have been hunting you these two hours; the boatswain is killed, Will Fry is wounded, and I am a prisoner; and if you do not yield, you are all lost." "Will they give us quarter then," says Tom Smith, "if we will yield?" "I will go ask," says Robinson; so he asked the captain, and the captain himself then calls out, "You, Smith, you know my voice; if you lay down your arms immediately, and submit, you shall have your lives, all but Will Atkins."

Upon this Will Atkins cried out, "For God's sake, Captain, give me quarter. They have all been as bad as I"; which was not true, for it seems this Will Atkins was the first man that laid hold of the captain when they mutinied, and used him barbarously, in tying his hands and giving him injurious language. However, the captain told him to lay down his arms and trust to the governor's mercy; by which he meant me, for they all called me governor. And so they all laid down their arms, and begged their lives. I sent the man that had parleyed with them, and two more, who bound them all; and then my great army of fifty men, which, with those three, were in all but eight, came up and seized upon them, and upon their boat; only I kept myself out of sight for reasons of state.

⊰⊱ CHAPTER 22 ⊰⊱

OUR next work was to repair the boat, and think of seizing the ship; and as for the captain, now he expostulated with his crew upon the villainy of their practices with him, and at length upon the further wickedness of their design, and how certainly it must bring them to misery and distress in the end, and perhaps to the gallows. They all appeared very penitent, and begged hard for their lives. As for that, he told them they were none of his prisoners, but the commander's of the island; that they thought they had set him on shore on a barren, uninhabited island; but it had pleased God so to direct them, that it was inhabited, and that the governor was an Englishman; that he might hang them all there, if he pleased; but as he had given them all quarter, he supposed he would send them to England to be dealt with there as justice required, except Atkins, whom he was commanded by the governor to advise to prepare for death, for that he would be hanged in the morning.

Though all this was a fiction of his own, yet it had its desired effect: Atkins fell upon his knees to beg the captain to intercede with the governor for his life; and all the rest begged of him, for God's sake, that they might not be sent to England.

It now occurred to me that the time of our deliverance was come, and that it would be easy to enlist these fellows in getting possession of the ship; so I remained in the dark from them, that they might not see what kind of a governor they had, and called the captain to me; when I called, as at a good distance, one of the men was ordered to speak again, and say to the captain, "Captain, the commander calls for you"; and the captain replied, "Tell his excellency I am coming." All believed that the commander was nearby with his fifty men. Upon the captain's coming to me, I told him my project for seizing the ship, which he liked wonderfully well, and resolved to put it in execution the next morning. But, in order to be more sure of success, I told him we must divide the prisoners, and that he should go and take Atkins and two more of the worst of them, and send them pinioned to the cave where the others lay. This was committed to Friday and the two men who came on shore with the captain. The others I ordered to my bower; and as it was fenced in, and they pinioned, the place was secure enough.

To these in the morning I sent the captain, who was to enter into a parley, and tell me whether he thought they might be trusted to go on board and surprise the ship. He talked to them of the injury done him, of the condition they were brought to, and that though the governor had given them quarter for their lives as to the present action, yet that, if they were sent to England, they would all be hanged in chains, to be sure; but if they would join in so just an attempt as to recover the ship, he would have the governor's engagement for their pardon.

Anyone may guess how readily such a proposal would be accepted by men in their condition; they fell down on their knees to the captain, and promised, with the deepest imprecations, that they would be faithful to him to the last drop, and that they should owe their lives to him, and would go with him all over the world, and would own him as a father as long as they lived. "Well," says the captain, "I must go and tell the governor what you say, and see what I can do to bring him to consent to it." So he brought me an account of the temper he found them in, and that he verily believed they would be faithful. However, that we might be very secure, I told him he should go back again and choose five of them, and tell them that he would take those five to be his assistants, and that the governor would keep the other two; and the five that were sent prisoners to the castle (my cave) as hostages; and that if they proved unfaithful, the five hostages should be hanged in chains alive on the shore. This looked severe, and convinced them that the governor was in earnest; however, they had no way left them but to accept it.

Our strength was now thus ordered for the expedition:
first, the captain, his mate, and passenger; second, the two
prisoners of the first gang, to whom, having their characters from the captain, I had given their liberty and trusted
them with arms; third, the other two that I had kept till
now in my bower pinioned but, on the captain's motion,
had now released; fourth, these five released at last; so that
they were twelve in all, besides the five we kept prisoners
in the cave for hostages.

I asked the captain if he was willing to venture with
these hands on board the ship. As for me and my man
Friday, I did not think it proper for us to stir, having seven
men left behind; it was employment enough for us to keep
them asunder, and supply them with victuals. As to the
five in the cave, Friday went in twice a day to them to
supply them with necessaries.

When I showed myself to the two in the bower, it was
with the captain, who told them I was the person the
governor had ordered to look after them; and that it was
the governor's pleasure that they should not stir anywhere
but by my direction; that if they did, they would be fetched
into the castle, and be laid in irons; so that, as we never
suffered them to see me as a governor, I now appeared as
another person, and spoke of the governor, the garrison,
the castle, and the like, upon all occasions.

The captain now had no difficulty before him but to
furnish his two boats, stop the breach of one, and man
them. He made his passenger captain of one, with four of

the men; and himself, his mate, and three more, went in the other; and they contrived their business very well, for they came up to the ship about midnight. As soon as they came within call of the ship, he made Robinson hail them, and tell them they had brought off the men and the boat, but that it was a long time before they had found them, and the like, holding them in a chat till they came to the ship's side; when the captain and the mate, going aboard first, with their arms, immediately knocked down the second mate and carpenter with the butt end of their muskets, being very faithfully seconded by their men; they secured all the rest that were upon the main and quarter decks, and began to fasten the hatches to keep them down that were below; when the other boat and their men, entering at the fore-chains, secured the forecastle of the ship, and the scuttle which went into the cookroom, making three men they found there prisoners. When this was done, and all safe upon deck, the captain ordered the mate, with three men, to break into the roundhouse, where the new rebel captain lay, who, having taken the alarm, had got up, and with two men and a boy had got firearms in their hands; and when the mate, with a crowbar, split open the door, the new captain and his men fired boldly among them, and wounded the mate and two of the men. The mate, calling for help, rushed into the roundhouse, wounded as he was, and with his pistol shot the new captain through the head, so that he never spoke a word more; upon which the rest yielded and the ship was taken.

As soon as the ship was thus secured, the captain ordered seven guns to be fired, which was the signal agreed upon with me to give me notice of his success, which you may be sure I was very glad to hear, having sat watching upon the shore for it till near two o'clock in the morning. Having thus heard the signal, I laid me down; and it having been a day of great fatigue, I slept very sound, till I was awakened by the noise of a gun; and starting up, I heard a man call, "Governor, Governor," and I knew the captain's voice. I climbed to the top of the hill, where he stood, and pointing to the ship, he embraced me in his arms. "My dear friend and deliverer," says he, "there's your ship, for she is all yours, and so are we, and all that belong to her." I cast my eyes to the ship, and there she rode within a little more than half a mile of the shore; for they had weighed her anchor as soon as they were masters of her and, the weather being fair, had brought her to just against the mouth of the creek; and the tide being up, the captain had landed just at my door. I was at first ready to sink down with surprise; for I saw my deliverance, indeed, visibly put into my hands, and a large ship just ready to carry me away whither I pleased to go; but as the captain had taken me in his arms, I held fast by him, or I should have fallen to the ground. He immediately pulled a bottle out of his pocket, and gave me a dram of cordial, which he had brought on purpose for me. After I drank it, I sat down upon the ground; and though it brought me to myself, yet it was a good while before I could speak.

The poor man said a thousand kind and tender things to me, to compose and bring me to myself; but such was the flood of joy in my breast that it put all my spirits into confusion; and at last it broke out into tears; I then embraced him, and we rejoiced together. I told him I looked upon him as a man sent from Heaven to deliver me, and that the whole transaction seemed to be a chain of wonders; that such things as these were the testimonies we had of a secret hand of Providence governing the world, and an evidence that the eye of an infinite power could search into the remotest corner of the world, and send help to the miserable whenever He pleased. I forgot not to lift up my heart in thankfulness to Heaven; and what heart could forbear to bless Him, who had in a miraculous manner provided for me in such a wilderness, and in such a desolate condition?

When we had talked awhile, the captain told me he had brought me some little refreshment, such as the ship afforded. Upon this he called aloud to the boat, and bade his men bring the things ashore that were for the governor. First, he gave me a case of bottles full of excellent cordial waters, six large bottles of Madeira wine, two pounds of excellent good tobacco, twelve good pieces of the ship's beef, and six pieces of pork, with a bag of peas, and about a hundredweight of biscuit; he also brought me a box of sugar, a box of flour, a bag full of lemons, and two bottles of lime juice, and abundance of other things. But, besides these, and what was a thousand times more useful to me, he brought me six new clean shirts, six very good neck-cloths, two pairs of gloves, one pair of shoes, a hat, and one pair of stockings, with a very good suit of clothes of his own, which had been worn but very little; in a word, he clothed me from head to foot. It was a very kind and agreeable present, as anyone may imagine, to one in my circumstances; but never was anything in the world of that kind so unpleasant, awkward, and uneasy, as it was to me to wear such clothes at first.

After these ceremonies were past, and after all his good things were brought into my little apartment, we began to consult what was to be done with the prisoners we had; for it was worth considering whether we might venture to take them away with us or no, especially two of them, whom we knew to be incorrigible to the last degree; and the captain said that, if he did carry them away, it must be in irons, as malefactors, to be delivered over to justice at the first English colony he could come at. Upon this I told him that, if he desired it, I would undertake to bring the two men he spoke of to make it their own request that he should leave them upon the island. "I should be very glad of that," says the captain, "with all my heart." So I caused Friday and the two released prisoners to go to the cave, and bring up the five men, pinioned, to the bower. After some time, I came thither dressed in my new habit; and now I was called governor again. I caused the men to be brought before me, and I told them I had got a full account of their villainous behavior to the captain, and how they had run away with the ship, but that they were fallen into the pit which they had dug for others. I let them know that by my direction the ship had been seized; that she lay now in the road; and they might see, by and by, that their new captain had received the reward of his villainy, and that they would see him hanging at the yardarm; that as to them, I wanted to know what they had to say why I should not execute them as pirates, taken in the fact, as by my commission they could not doubt but I had authority so to do.

One of them answered in the name of the rest that they had nothing to say but this, that when they were taken, the captain promised them their lives, and they humbly implored my mercy. But I told them I knew not what mercy to show them; for I had resolved to quit the island with all my men, and had taken passage with the captain for England; and the captain could not carry them to England other than as prisoners, in irons, to be tried for mutiny, the consequence of which would be the gallows; so that I could not tell what was best for them, unless they had a mind to take their fate in the island; if they desired that, I had some inclination to give them their lives. They seemed very thankful for it, and said they would much rather venture to stay there than be carried to England to be hanged.

I accordingly set them at liberty, and bade them retire into the woods to the place whence they came, and I would leave them some firearms, some ammunition, and some directions how they should live very well. Upon this I told the captain I would stay that night to prepare my

DANIEL DEFOE

things, and desired him to go on board in the meantime, and keep all right in the ship, and send the boat on shore next day for me; ordering him to cause the new captain, who was killed, to be hanged at the yardarm, that these men might see him.

When the captain was gone, I sent for the men again, and I told them I thought they had made a right choice. I then told them I would put them into the way of making it easy to them; accordingly, I gave them the whole history of the place, and of my coming to it; showed them my fortifications, the way I made my bread, planted my grain, cured my grapes; and, in a word, all that was necessary to make them easy. I told them the story also of the seventeen Spaniards that were to be expected, for whom I left a letter, and made them promise to treat them in common with themselves.

I left them my five muskets, three fowling pieces, three swords, and a barrel and a half of powder. I gave them a description of the way I managed the goats, and directions to milk and fatten them, and to make both butter and cheese. I should prevail with the captain to leave them two barrels of gunpowder more, and some garden seeds, which I told them I would have been very glad of; also I gave them the bag of peas which the captain had brought me to eat, and bade them be sure to sow and increase them.

Having done all this, I left them the next day, and went on board the ship. The next morning early, two of the five men came swimming to the ship's side and, making a most lamentable complaint of the other three, begged to be taken into the ship, for God's sake, for they should be murdered, and begged the captain to take them on board. After their solemn promises of amendment, they were taken on board and were soundly whipped and pickled, after which they proved very honest and quiet fellows.

Some time after this, the boat was ordered on shore with the things promised to the men; to which the captain, at my intercession, caused their chests and clothes to be added, which they took, and were very thankful for.

When I took leave of this island, I carried on board, for relics, the great goatskin cap I had made, my umbrella, and one parrot; also I forgot not to take the money I formerly mentioned, which had laid by me so long useless that it was grown tarnished, and could hardly pass for silver till it had been a little rubbed and handled; as also the money I found in the wreck of the Spanish ship. And thus I left the island, the 19th of December, as I found by the ship's account, in the year 1686, after I had been upon it seven and twenty years, two months, and nineteen days; being delivered from this second captivity the same day of the month that I first made my escape in the longboat from among the Moors of Sallee. In this vessel, after a long voyage, I arrived in England the 11th of June, in the year 1687, having been thirty-five years absent.

~ 249 ~

❀ CHAPTER 23 ❀

WHEN I came to England, I was as perfect a stranger to all the world as if I had never been known there. I went down into Yorkshire; but my father and mother were dead, and all the family extinct, except that I found two of the children of one of my brothers; and as I had been long ago given over for dead, there had been no provision made for me; so that, in a word, I found nothing to relieve or assist me; and the money I had would not do much for me as to settling in the world. So I resolved to go to Lisbon, and see if I might not come by some information of the state of my plantation in the Brazils, and of what was become of my partner. With this view I took shipping for Lisbon, where I arrived in April following, my man Friday accompanying me very honestly in all these ramblings and proving a most faithful servant upon all occasions. When I came to Lisbon, I found out, by inquiry, my old friend the captain of the ship who first took me up at sea off the shore of Africa. He was now grown old and did not know me, but I soon brought myself to his remembrance.

After some passionate expressions of the old acquaintance between us, the old man told me he had not been in the Brazils for about nine years but that he could assure me that when he came away, my partner was living; and that he believed I would have a very good account of the improvement of the plantation; for that, upon the general belief of my being cast away and drowned, my trustees had given in my part of the plantation to the procurator fiscal, who had appropriated it in case I never came to claim it, one third to the king, and two thirds to the monastery of St. Augustine, to be expended for the benefit of the poor; but that if I appeared to claim the inheritance, it would be restored.

The old man then told me there were ships in the river of Lisbon just ready to go away to Brazil; and he made me enter my name in a public register, with his affidavit, affirming upon oath that I was alive, and that I was the same person who took up the land for the planting the said plantation at first. This being regularly attested by a notary, he directed me to send it, with a letter of his writing, to a merchant of his acquaintance at the place, and then proposed my staying with him till an account came of the return.

Never was anything more honorable than these proceedings; for in less than seven months I received a letter from my partner, congratulating me very affectionately upon my being alive, and inviting me very passionately to come over and take possession of my own; and, in the meantime, to give him orders to whom he should deliver my effects if I did not come myself. He sent me, as a present, five chests of excellent sweetmeats, and a hundred pieces of gold uncoined. The two merchants for whose account I had gone to sea had died, but their trustees shipped me, by the same fleet, one thousand two hundred chests of sugar, eight hundred rolls of tobacco, and the rest of my account in gold.

I might well say now, indeed, that the latter end of Job was better than the beginning. It is impossible to express the flutterings of my heart when I found all my wealth about me. In a word, I turned pale and grew sick; and had not the old man run and fetched me a cordial, I believe the sudden surprise of joy had overset Nature, and I had died upon the spot.

I was now master, all on a sudden, of above five thousand pounds sterling in money, and had an estate in the Brazils of above a thousand pounds a year, as sure as an estate of lands in England; and, in a word, I was in a condition which I scarce knew how to understand, or how to compose myself for the enjoyment of it. The first thing I did was to recompense my original benefactor, my good old captain. I caused a procuration to be drawn, granting one hundred moidores a year to him during his life, and fifty moidores a year to his son after him, for his life; and thus I requited my old man.

I was now to consider which way to steer my course next, and what to do with the estate that Providence had thus put into my hands; and, indeed, I had more care upon my head now than I had in my silent state of life in the island, where I wanted nothing but what I had, and had nothing but what I wanted; whereas I had now a great charge upon me, and my business was how to secure it. I had never a cave now to hide my money in, or a place where it might lie without lock or key, till it grew moldy and tarnished before anybody would meddle with it. After much reflection, I resolved to return to England with it, where I concluded I should find some relations that would be faithful to me.

Having sold my cargo, and turned all my effects into good bills of exchange, my next difficulty was which way to go to England: I had been accustomed enough to the sea, and yet I had a strange aversion to go to England by sea at that time; and though I could give no reason for it, yet I resolved to travel all the way by land; which, as I was not in haste, and did not value the charge, was by much the pleasanter way; and to make it more so, my old captain brought an English gentleman, the son of a merchant in Lisbon, who was willing to travel with me; after which we picked up two more English merchants also, and two young Portuguese gentlemen; so that in all there were six of us, and five servants, including my man Friday.

In this manner I set out from Lisbon; and our company being very well mounted and armed, we made a little troop, whereof they did me the honor to call me captain, because I was the oldest man. I shall not trouble you now with my land journal; but some adventures that happened to us in this difficult journey I must not omit.

We crossed to Spain, and about the middle of October, we came to the province of Navarre. There we were alarmed, at several towns, with an account that so much snow was fallen on the French side of the mountains that several travelers were obliged to come back to Pampeluna, after having attempted to pass on.

When we came to Pampeluna itself, we found it so, indeed; and to me, that had become used to a hot climate, and to countries where I could scarce bear any clothes on, the cold was insufferable: nor was it more painful than surprising to come but ten days before out of central Spain, where the weather was very hot, and immediately to feel a wind from the Pyrenean Mountains, so very keen, so severely cold, as to benumb our fingers and toes.

Poor Friday was really frightened when he saw the mountains all covered with snow, and felt cold weather, which he had never seen or felt before in his life. At Pampeluna it continued snowing with so much violence that the people said winter was come before its time, and the roads were now quite impassable. We had been no less than twenty days at Pampeluna when we found a guide, who told us he would undertake to carry us into France with no hazard from the snow, provided we were armed sufficiently to protect ourselves from wild beasts; for, he said, upon these great snows it was frequent for some wolves to show themselves at the foot of the mountains, being made ravenous for want of food, the ground being covered with snow. We told him we were well enough prepared for such creatures and accordingly set out from Pampeluna on the 15th of November; and, instead of going forward, he came directly back with us on the same road we had come, about twenty miles; when, having passed two rivers, and come into the plain country, we found ourselves in a warm climate again, where the country was pleasant, and no snow to be seen; but on a sudden turning to his left, he approached the mountains another way, and he made so many meanders, and led us by such winding ways, that we insensibly passed the height of the mountains without being much encumbered with the snow; and, all on a sudden, he showed us the pleasant fruitful provinces of Languedoc and Gascony, all green and flourishing, though at a great distance.

We now began to descend every day, and to come more north than before; and so, depending upon our guide, we went on.

IT WAS about two hours before night when, our guide being something before us and not quite in sight, out-rushed three monstrous wolves, and after them a bear, from a hollow way adjoining to a thick wood; one of the wolves made at the guide and attacked him with such violence that he had not time to draw his pistol but hallooed and cried out to us most lustily. I bade my man Friday ride up, and see what was the matter. As soon as Friday came in sight of the man, he hallooed out, "O Master! O Master!" but, like a bold fellow, rode directly up to the poor man, and with his pistol shot the wolf in the head.

But it was enough to have terrified a bolder man than I, and, indeed, it alarmed all our company, when, with the noise of Friday's pistol, we heard on both sides the most dismal howling of wolves, and the noise was redoubled by the echo of the mountains.

We all mended our pace, and rode up as fast as we could to see what was the matter. As soon as we came clear of the trees, which blinded us before, we saw clearly how Friday had disengaged the poor guide. But the man was most hurt; for the raging creature had bit him twice, once in the arm, and another time a little above his knee.

We were still in a wild place, and what to do we hardly knew; the howling of wolves ran much in my head; and, indeed, except the noise I once heard on the shore of Africa, I never heard anything that filled me with so much horror. But we had near three leagues to go, and our guide hastened us, so we went forward on our journey.

The ground was still covered with snow, though not so deep and dangerous as on the mountains; and the ravenous creatures, as we heard afterwards, were come down into the forest and plain country, pressed by hunger, to seek for food, and had done a great deal of mischief in the villages, where they killed a great many sheep and horses, and some people too. We had one dangerous place to pass, of which our guide told us, if there were more wolves in the country, we should find them there; and this was a small plain, surrounded with woods on every side, and a long narrow lane, which we were to pass to get through the wood, and then we should come to the village where we were to lodge. We met with nothing in the plain, but when we came to the wood, through which we were to pass, we saw a confused number of wolves standing just at the entrance. Near the entrance, there lay some large timber trees, which had been cut down the summer before, and I suppose lay there for carriage. I drew my little troop in among those trees, and placing ourselves in a line behind one long tree, I advised them all to alight, and keeping that tree before us for a breastwork, to stand in a triangle or three fronts enclosing our horses in the center. We did so, and it was well we did; for never was a more furious charge than the creatures made upon us in this place. They came on with a growling kind of noise, and mounted the piece of timber, which was our breastwork. I ordered our men to fire, every other man, and they took their aim so sure that they killed several of the wolves at the first volley; but there was a necessity to keep a continual firing, for they came on like devils, those behind pushing on those before.

I was loath to spend our shot too hastily; so I called one of the men, and giving him a horn of powder, I bade him lay a train all along the piece of timber. He did so; and had but just time to get away, when the wolves came up to it, and some got upon it, when I, snapping an uncharged pistol close to the powder, set it on fire; those that were upon the timber were scorched, and six or seven of them fell or rather jumped in among us, with the force and fright of the fire; we dispatched these in an instant, and the rest were so frightened with the light, which the night, for it was now very near dark, made more terrible, that they drew back a little; upon which I ordered our last pistols to be fired off in one volley, and after that we gave a shout. Upon this the wolves turned tail, and we sallied immediately upon near twenty lame ones, that we found struggling on the ground, and fell a-cutting them with our swords, which answered our expectation; for the crying and howling they made was understood by their fellows; so that they all fled and left us.

The field of battle being thus cleared, we made forward again, for we had still near a league to go. We heard the ravenous creatures howl in the woods as we went, several times, and sometimes we fancied we saw some of them, but we were not certain; in about an hour more we came to the town where we were to lodge, which we found all in arms; for, it seems, the night before, the wolves and some bears had broke into the village and put them in such terror that they were obliged to keep guard night and day to preserve their cattle and, indeed, their people.

The next morning our guide's limbs swelled so much with the rankling of his two wounds, that he could go no farther; so we were obliged to take a new guide here, and go to Toulouse, where we found a warm climate, a fruitful pleasant country, and no snow, no wolves, nor anything like them. But, for my part, I shall never care to cross those mountains again; I would rather go a thousand leagues by sea, though I was sure to meet with a storm once a week.

I have nothing uncommon to take notice of in my passage through France. I traveled from Toulouse to Paris, and without any considerable stay came to Calais, and landed safe at Dover, the 14th of January. I was now come to the center of my travels, and had in a little time all my new discovered estate safe about me.

I now resolved to dispose of my plantation in the Brazils, and for this purpose I wrote to my old friend at Lisbon, who offered it to the two merchants who were the survivors of my trustees. They accepted the offer, and remitted thirty-three thousand pieces of eight to my friend to pay for it; he then sent me bills of exchange for this amount.

Though I had sold my estate in the Brazils, yet I could not keep the country out of my head; nor could I resist the strong inclination I had to see my island. Yet for almost seven years I did not run abroad, during which time I took my two nephews, the children of one of my brothers, into my care; the eldest having something of his own, I bred up as a gentleman, and gave him a settlement of some addition to his estate after my decease. Finding the other a sensible, bold, enterprising young fellow, I put him into a good ship, and sent him to sea; and this young fellow afterwards drew me in, old as I was, to further adventures myself.

In the meantime, I in part settled myself here; for, first of all, I married, and that not either to my disadvantage or dissatisfaction, and had three children, two sons and one daughter; but my wife dying, and my nephew coming home with good success from a voyage to Spain, my inclination to go abroad and his importunity prevailed, and engaged me to go in his ship as a private trader to the East Indies: this was in the year 1694.

But these things, with some very surprising incidents in some new adventures of my own, for ten years more, I may perhaps give a further account of hereafter.

DANIEL DEFOE

⌒

Although never shipwrecked on a deserted island, Daniel Defoe was, like his unforgettable hero Robinson Crusoe, often forced to live by his wits. A prodigiously energetic, creative—and controversial—figure in his day, Defoe managed to sample about as much of life as could be sampled by any one man. Born in 1660, the son of a London butcher, he trained for the Presbyterian ministry—a career plan he abandoned—married early, and had a large family.

In the absence of a religious calling, Defoe embraced commerce with gusto and traded (mostly unsuccessfully) in wine, tobacco, hosiery, bricks, and perfume. Before he died of a "lethargy" in a London rooming house in 1731, Defoe had sampled prison and the pillory (for his anti-establishment beliefs), had been a soldier, a spy, a journalist, and a publisher, as well as the author of some 500 books on topics ranging from politics to etiquette and the occult.

His most famous fiction, *Robinson Crusoe*, was based on the actual adventures of a Scottish sailor, Alexander Selkirk, who marooned himself for over four years with little more than goats for company on an island off the coast of Chile.

In addition to *Robinson Crusoe*, Defoe is best remembered today for two other supreme works of creative spirit, *Moll Flanders* and *A Journal of the Plague Year*.